Easier said than Done!

Adventures in the Language Business

John M. Taplin

Introduction

I wish I'd taken a picture! My doorbell rang and within moments two cheerful, summer-tanned people were unpacking wine glasses and cool prosecco, then leaning against my kitchen bar while radiating health and positivity. We were in one of the breaks from the Covid pandemic. (Yes, we were all double vaxxed and wearing masks in public places.) My 2021 life was coloured with un-packed boxes from my recent move and an almost total lack of face-to-face interaction with other humans. This was a rare and memorable get together. Literally and metaphorically, all the windows and doors were open. Fresh Alberta sun and air danced through my new home. This was when I met Cathie and John for the first time.

The pandemic raged on; we all lost friends, colleagues, businesses, and family during this time. We witnessed the continued collapse of international travel and English language education. John kept writing. We held weekly meetings over Zoom to narrow in on the topic; and story-editing was all by email. John kept writing!

We needed to develop a storyline and in doing so, we found things in common. For those in the business, you'll understand when I say that years earlier, I completed my four-week CELTA boot camp at Global Village Calgary — John's school. I went on to teach with U of C, city libraries, and LINC. While I was working with John's manuscript, I was teaching the University Pathways program on-line, for Stafford House. The meaning of time passing, going to work, collegial relationships, family times, going shopping — the meaning of everything was shaken and being rearranged.

Once we had three or four tidy chapters, we reached out to some industry friends to see if they would join the project as first readers. They were an important part of our process and gave us valuable input. On the back cover you will see some short remarks from Linda Auzins (Languages Canada) and Tania Knoch (Global Village Calgary and Victoria). We also connected with Cath D'Amico (Trent International) and Justin Quinn (Centre for English Studies). Both were very encouraging and made the case for reflections on crisis management, host training, cultural preparation for students, and of course, family life. We are grateful to these first readers for helping us chart our course!

I didn't see Cathie and John until months later. John and I had a socially distanced meeting in his studio/garage that overlooked their snowy Calgary backyard. We shared a wonderful meal, the three of us — then it was back to our pandemic routines. They went off to the Okanagan in British Columbia while I settled in for the cold weather in Calgary's Sunnyside.

Although the pandemic restrictions are easing, world tensions are rising. The Russian invasion of Ukraine leads the hourly news. I am reminded of all my English language students and the stories they've shared; students from Ukraine, Kazakhstan, Syria, Afghanistan, Pakistan, Columbia, Brazil, Venezuela, Mexico and Turkey (among others). It is to these students — and the spirit of international education and language learning — that I dedicate my efforts on this project.

Sally

Sally V. Truss
Calgary, Alberta
March 13, 2022

For Cathie

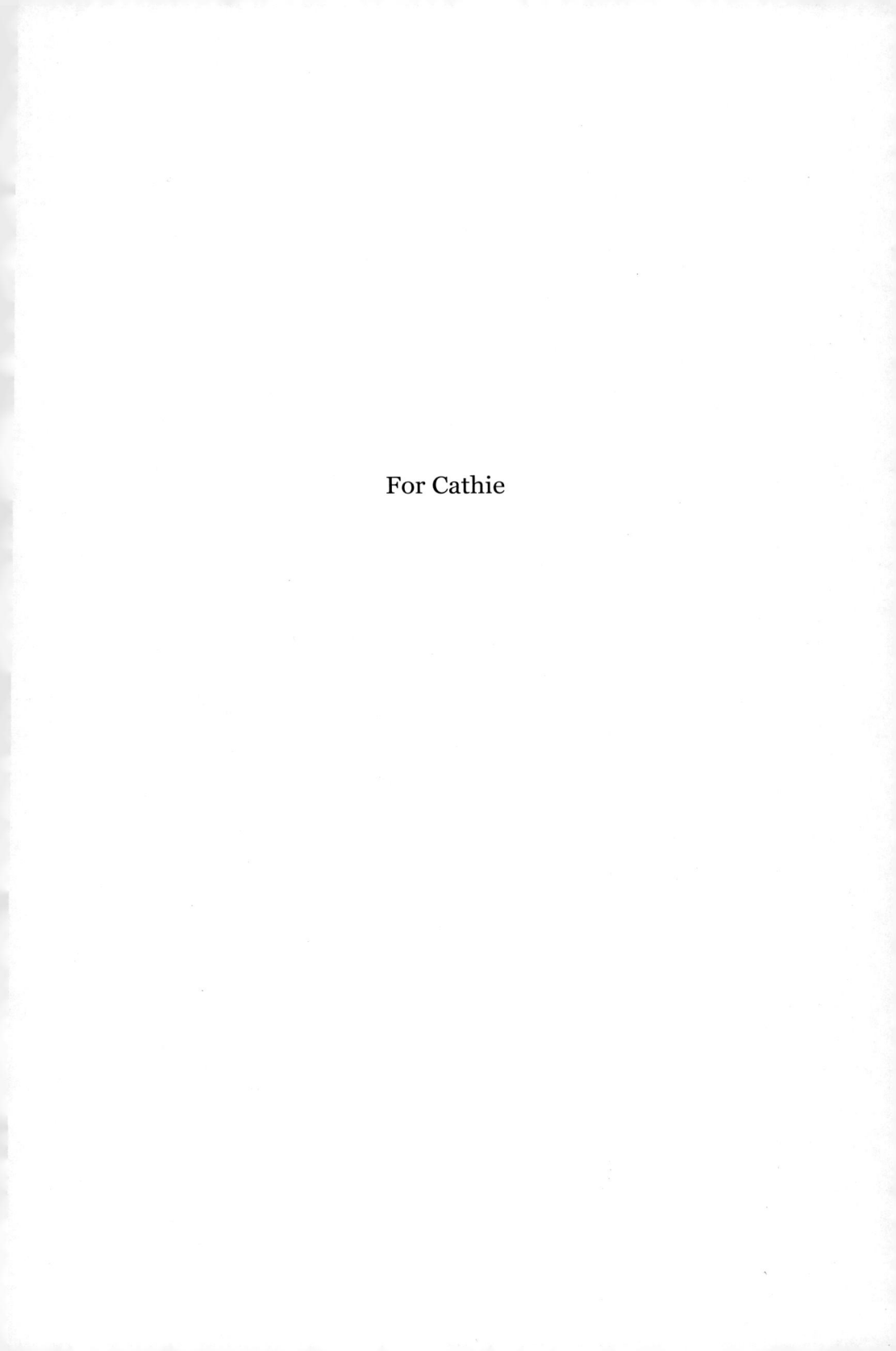

PROJECT TEAM

Project manager and story-editor — Sally Truss

Copy Editor — Ena Spalding

Design and print production — Jackie Bourgaize

Copyright 2022, John M. Taplin

First print-edition, 2022

All rights reserved. No part of this publication may be reproduced, stored in a retrieval system, or transmitted in any form or by any means, electronic, mechanical, photocopying, recording, or otherwise, without written permission of the author and publisher.

Published by:

    Sally Truss
    SierraVTango Enterprises
    Calgary, Alberta, Canada

Contents

Early Influences 9
A High School Teacher 13
A Fish Out of Water 19
A University Language Program 29
Japanese Student Exchange 41
School Start-up 47
Adult Homestay 59
Youth Programs 67
Relocating the School 73
Team Vibrations 85
Marketing Ups and Downs 95
Global Citizens 111
Buckle Up! 123
Wellness and Safety 131
2020 141
Lessons Learned from Students 155
Afterword 165
Acknowledgements 167
Selected Bibliography 169

8 Easier Said Than Done

Early Influences

Walking down the airplane steps onto the tarmac in Denpasar, Bali, I was a mixture of emotions. At 24 years of age, I was taking my first steps outside my native Australia. It was like setting foot on a new world. As I breathed in, I could almost taste the thick humidity. Steam rose from the pavement as the afternoon sun shone brightly on the fresh aftermath of a tropical rainstorm.

Hot, humid weather pervaded many months of the year in the state of New South Wales where I lived. But now, arriving in Indonesia in the rainy season, the proximity to the Equator was evident. We had flown low over jungle clinging to the fringe of the island's coast on our landing approach. Inside the airport, the smell of clove cigarettes infused the air. Unmistakably, I was somewhere other than Australia.

Travelling alone, I drank in the sights and sounds. The disquieting feelings of homesickness passed after the first few days. Two weeks had initially felt like a long time to be separated from my life in Australia. With a flash of insight, I realized that Bali was a haven where I could reflect on many opportunities for learning if I just remained open to whatever happened.

I was suffering from neck pain from whiplash injuries, so I sought out the cheap but effective massages available at the beach. I met a local woman of about 50, who was remarkably skilled. After an hour lying out in the open on the beach, with the nimble ministration of her hands, I felt better than I had in years. This turned into a daily routine while I remained in the Kuta area.

The woman taught me words and expressions in Bahasa Indonesian (the official language of Indonesia) and explained local customs in her fractured English. When I remarked that it was generally only tourists who went any distance into the water at the beach, she said that most locals were afraid to venture out because many Balinese Hindus believed that evil spirits inhabited the depths. She added that some Hindus believed in the healing powers of the ocean and others acknowledged both the positive as well as negative spirts associated with the mysteries of large bodies of water. Having been brought up Christian, and with limited cross-cultural experience, I thought at first that her Hindu devotion was built on superstition. However, she had a peace about her. It became clear to me that her religion helped her maintain a serene outlook on the world.

She also had a quiet, humorous way of accepting things. As someone raised in Aussie beach culture, I was accustomed to swimming in the ocean. She merely tsked and smiled resignedly when I sat back down on my beach towel on the sand.

One day there was a funeral on the beach with a long procession of Balinese dressed in white and carrying a shrouded coffin on a wooden trestle. I watched, fascinated. Again, I was struck by the dignity in the way the locals went about things.

When my beach masseuse-turned-guide invited me to her family home in the back streets of Kuta, I accepted. Huddled in a cramped courtyard, drinking tea with family members and their friends from many generations was one of the highlights of the trip.

From a very young age, I was intrigued by different cultures and observing how people interact. My father was a Baptist minister in the early 1960s in Griffith, a town about 570 kilometres west of Sydney. He took me along on visits to rural Indigenous settlements before I was old enough to start school. I remember the faces of the men, women and children, framed by black, wiry hair and lined with the ravages of the hot climate and the travails of their lives. They sat warily outside their humpies, which were just flimsy shelters with wooden supports precariously holding sheets of tin siding together.

There was always a fire going, even in the hottest weather, and they would offer tea in tin cups, which we would all drink while my father asked how they were getting along. We sat cross-legged on the ground with them, shooing away the flies and the smoke from the fire. This early memory of community has stayed with me. I noticed that the people we visited had almost nothing material. Dad reminded me that they had each other and showed respect to each other and to "whitefellas" like my father, who took an interest in them.

When I was seven years old in 1964, a black preacher from the southern United States came to our country town. Among the reasons he stands out in my memory are his bonhomie and inquisitiveness about what was going on in our very conservative place. People were taken with the charismatic preacher.

My sister Ann, who was four at the time, commented that he was very black. Rev. Wallace Hartsfield was not disarmed by the honest curiosity of a small child. He jokingly showed her the inside of his hands, which were much lighter. He stayed in our home for about a week. His presence provided an insight that remains with me today. Even though we can look at someone from another ethnic group or culture as different, when we get to know them even just a little, the mystique of race falls away and we remember them as characteristic individuals. From such early influences began my passion for teaching and learning, exploring and later building a language business.

TIPS

If you are a teacher or an administrative staff member:

- Reflect on your personal history and what values inspired you to become involved in education
- Consider what role early adventures, influences and interests play in the stories of your colleagues and students

If you are a manager:

- Both of the above, and
- Ask potential hires about their experiences to gain a sense of their values

A High School Teacher

When the 1982 school year started, the head of the English Department at Kempsey High School in the Australian state of New South Wales told me that we had to add a weekly lesson of Asian languages to the Grade 7 curriculum. Since I had just been in Bali, he appointed me to teach the Bahasa Indonesian class.

I objected, saying that I could hardly speak any of the language. When I added that all I had to contribute were photos and mementoes of the trip, the English Head replied, "That's fine, mate. Teach the kids some cultural stuff and throw in some Indonesian vocabulary."

I soon came to enjoy teaching the class. The kids responded well. Years later, I returned to Kempsey where I ran into a former student. I had taught her English for at least a year for four hours a week. But what she remembered was the once-a-week Indonesian class.

When I arrived as a newly-minted teacher at Kempsey High School, there were mixed perspectives about teaching and learning. The students in years seven to twelve (equivalent to Grades 7 to 12 in Canada) were a mix of Indigenous and non-Indigenous. While a few teachers were openly antagonistic to some of the kids, most were there to do their best to help them. However, discipline in classes was a huge concern.

Having been through my own school of hard knocks for six years at Epping Boys' High in Sydney from 1970 to 1975, I had salutary lessons in what to do and what not to do as a teacher. In my experience, the teachers who had fared badly, lost the respect of students and even in some cases engaged aggressively with the all-boy classes, had usually fallen victim to letting students get a rise out of them. I was determined not to swallow the bait.

I did not have to wait long for my first real test. It was the first Friday of term on a hot, humid day in early February. I was teaching 10E7 in period eight, the dreaded final 40 minutes of the school week when all were waiting for the school bell to ring at 3:17 p.m. to signal the start of the weekend. The class of twenty 15 and 16-year-olds and I had warily circled each other all week. They were sizing me up as the rookie teacher with the shoulder-length hair and scrappy beard.

With just a few minutes to go in the lesson, I noticed that one student at the back was sitting there vacantly. I should have just left him alone. Rodney was a tough-looking kid who, I was to find out, was a star of the school's rugby league team. I asked him to bring his workbook up to the front of the classroom so I could see what he had been doing. He glared back at me. The rest of the class put their pens down, crossed their arms and waited for the show.

Rodney picked up his wooden desk, hoisted it above his head and hurled it against the exterior brick wall of the classroom, just below the high windows. The desk splintered into pieces that clattered against the hard floor. This was to be my defining moment. I had been teaching for less than week.

"A simple no would have done," I said evenly.

Fortunately, that defused the situation. The tension of the awkward, silent moment that followed was cut by the clanging school bell. The students rushed away. We were all free until Monday. I was to fail other tests of my patience over the four years at Kempsey High School, but it was critical that I passed the first one.

My goal was to keep students engaged and navigate around the inevitable discipline issues. I racked my brain for things that would interest them. Shakespeare was not going to cut it. Many of the novels and plays on the curriculum did not provoke interest, although *Lord of the Flies*[1] resonated with the teens.

---

1   William Golding, *Lord of the Flies* (1954)

During those Kempsey years, I spent many evenings with music playing in the background, trying to come up with lesson ideas. I decided to combine two of my preoccupations: the solace of listening to music and the challenge of preparing interesting lessons. It carried over successfully, at least at a minimum level. For 10E7, printing off the words to songs, playing the music and then setting comprehension questions led to better engagement from the class. I essentially dangled these music-centred lessons in front of the class once a week as a bribe, a reward for good behaviour.

Pink Floyd's *The Wall*[2] was popular at the time. The students often delighted in singing out loud along with the words of songs, especially with "We don't need no education". When the song got to the stage of "Teacher, leave those kids alone!" the class sang out loudly and the students collectively put an extra accusatory edge on the words while all staring at me in amusement. It was at this point that the Deputy Headmaster knocked on the door and walked in. The class and I thought I was in for a public dressing-down.

"Mr. Taplin, may I ask what you are doing with this class?"

"Well, Mr. Moroney, we are doing a listening and reading comprehension on a popular music theme," I answered.

"Keep up the good work," he said with a slightly bemused grimace. He left just a trace of dark sarcasm in the classroom. I exhaled in relief.

When I had started teaching 10E7, other teachers said, "Make sure you stay on the right side of Ivy."

Ivy was a physically-imposing Indigenous girl, captain of the netball team and clearly a leader in the community. One day she gave a backhander to John, a thin non-Indigenous boy, who acted as the class clown. He often swung back on his chair and,

---

2   Pink Floyd, *The Wall* (1979)

on this occasion, Ivy swung her arm back, landing a relatively light but strategically placed swipe across his chest. That sent him cartwheeling backwards off his chair. Jumping to his feet, he remonstrated with me, "Did you see that, sir?"

"See what?" I replied.

Like other teachers at Kempsey High, I had to deal with volatile situations on the fly and try to maintain a reasonably firm hand. Humour helped to defuse situations.

Throughout my time in the classroom at Kempsey High School, even though it was heavy going at times, my interest in multiculturalism grew, especially because of my trip to Bali. From my earliest days training as a teacher, I saw the classroom as a microcosm of relationships in the world outside. I could see those multicultural interactions worked better when people tried to understand and appreciate the different beliefs and customs of others. It became clear to me that any class I taught would involve negotiations among people with different perspectives, cultural and otherwise. As a high-school teacher in Australia, I was keenly aware that I needed to check my own assumptions constantly.

TIPS

If you are a teacher:

- Remember your own student experiences and utilize lessons learned in your teaching practice
- Use humour to build a positive classroom atmosphere and to defuse volatile situations
- Negotiate the curriculum by adapting teaching content and practice to students' interests and skill levels
- Navigate with sensitivity and awareness the different cultural and other perspectives of your students

18 Easier Said Than Done

A Fish Out of Water

Travelling to Bali and teaching at a high school in an Australian country town gave me an appreciation of what it feels like to be a fish out of water. Those transformational experiences helped me to be patient and flexible when I felt like a stranger during my first years in Canada. I believe they also made me more empathetic as my career in education developed and I taught and worked with students who were far from their home countries.

An introduction to Cathie, a Canadian visitor to the Australian town where I was teaching, was the defining event of my very fortunate life. Cathie was travelling on a work visa and had a job as a physiotherapist for one year at the local hospital. We were introduced by mutual friends. Not only did sparks fly, but we soon discovered that we shared a similar liberal view of the world and a thirst for adventure. We fell head over heels and just four months after meeting, we married on October 1, 1983.

Leaving our jobs and house in rural Australia, we flew to Calgary in Canada on May 6, 1984. Although I had been granted landed immigrant status, I did not envisage that I would make a permanent life in Canada. I officially became Canadian 20 years later when Australia allowed its citizens to become citizens of other countries as well.

Cathie settled into her physiotherapy career in the province of Alberta. My Australian qualifications meant I would have to go back to university if I wanted to teach in Alberta. I was quite sure I wanted to move into teaching adults English as a Second Language (ESL). I enrolled in courses at the University of Calgary. Initially I found the idea of depending on Cathie as the income earner and going back to university at 27 years old rather depressing. But there were few other options. Years later, I recognized that moving to Canada and taking up university studies again were my best career moves.

At first, I felt out of my depth in the Teaching English as a Second Language (TESL) diploma program. I knuckled down, completed the TESL Diploma in Curriculum and Instruction and secured a place in the master's program, also in the Faculty of Education in 1985. My specialty area of study was educational administration related to the field of teaching ESL. I focussed on the historical context of ESL in Canada (primarily Alberta) as a response to immigration, with an emphasis on Indo-Chinese refugees. These were "the boat people", who fled by boats after the end of the Vietnam War in 1975. Many immigrated to Australia, Canada and the United States starting in 1978, after spending years in refugee camps.

I was in Canada for over 18 months before I was paid as a teacher. I earned a little working on Cathie's family's farm (for which I proved unsuited) and received some research funding for graduate students. I supplemented my studies by volunteering with the Vietnamese Youth at Risk Program where I worked with male students in their late teens, who had received little formal schooling in refugee camps. Some were barely literate in their native language. After moving to Canada, they were in danger of drifting into gangs in cities like Calgary. English language skills held the key for them to gain useful employment and to keep out of trouble.

The students bore emotional scars and found their lives as "New Canadians" very challenging. I sought ways to engage them in learning English that would be practical for them. I found out that they enjoyed window-shopping and looking around stores, especially in malls. There they had the freedom to move around in the warmth, which was comfortable compared to the cold outside. They told me that they didn't know what to say when approached by salespeople.

One day, I borrowed my father-in-law's large twin-cab truck with ample room for the class of six students and headed off to The Brick department store for a field trip. The students were impressed by the effective expression, "No thanks, I'm just looking." It was a practical lesson, put to immediate use.

Driving back into the core of downtown Calgary with my small class, I was pulled over by a policeman with a radar gun. The students' eyes opened wide at this interaction. They were initially fearful of the uniformed officer. I put this down to the negative reputation of authority figures in their country. The policeman wrote out a ticket, advised me to check my speed and wished me a good day. It was an insight for the students into Canadian civility. For the rest of the term, I had a protracted battle with them as they insisted on collectively paying the $35 speeding fine. At the end of the term, they gave me a gift and waited for my reaction.

"Let me guess," I joked. "It cost 35 dollars." The students beamed back at me, collectively getting the last laugh.

In January 1986, I started teaching adult ESL classes several evenings a week and on Saturday mornings, in Calgary. I met inspiring people who, despite their many hardships, came to class with impressive reserves of goodwill and positive energy. Many had fled war in Vietnam, Cambodia, Laos, Nicaragua and El Salvador or had left behind conflicts in countries scattered around Europe, Africa and the Middle East. They often worked night shift as janitors or in service jobs at gas stations and convenience stores, while the rest of the city slept. Nevertheless, they would find the stamina to travel on public transit across the city in freezing conditions to make it to class.

As I was an immigrant to Canada myself and because I was thinking about how immigrants adjust to life in Alberta in my university work, I knew how easy I had it. Even when I had a setback, I could regroup with my English language skills. Cathie was earning a good income and I had a supportive Canadian extended family, even if they still made fun of my Aussie accent and my impaired ability to cope with the cold.

I tried to imagine the journey and upheaval of students and their families who were uprooted by profound events like the Vietnam War. Themes to do with assimilation, integration and multiculturalism coalesced in my master's thesis.

My first three years in Canada were busy, full of interesting people and new life lessons. Cathie and I travelled to London, as well as to Holland, Belgium, France, Spain and Italy with our friends, John and Gail, for six weeks in the summer of 1985. All these experiences, as well as learning from John Wilson about his English as a Foreign Language (EFL) teaching experience with adults, motivated me and gave impetus to my career in the field of English language teaching.

Then our first son, John George, was born in April 1986. We marvelled at our good fortune. Life continued to change.

Wondering if our future lives and careers lay in Canada or Australia, we decided on a six-month sojourn down under to see where the journey would take us. We left Calgary in September 1987 for Sydney where I worked as an EFL teacher. I found out that the Australian College of English (ACE) in Bondi Junction had some openings for part-time teaching jobs. They preferred to hire people who had come though their own Royal Society of Arts (RSA) training courses, the forerunners of the Certificate in English Language Teaching to Adults (CELTA) and the Diploma in English Language Teaching to Adults (DELTA), which I hadn't done.

My friend John Wilson helped me navigate the interview process and plan for lessons. I was contracted to teach an intermediate EFL class for three hours each morning. I felt like an infiltrator and soon I was being treated like one. The senior staff who managed teachers and supervised teaching practice ran a tight ship. Knowing that I had not taken the RSA program and ironically referring to me as "The Canadian", they kept a close eye on me.

In fact, the Teacher Training Manager had her desk set up right outside my classroom. I was in a fishbowl through which she saw what was going on and listened to hear if I was committing one of the cardinal sins of "too much teacher talk".

At 30 years old, I was a bit older than the other newer teachers, who like me still had to pay their dues. These teachers complained to me about how they were treated in terms of pay and lack of recognition of preparation time, that persistent chestnut in the working conditions of teachers. I was not touching staffroom politics with a ten-foot barge pole, though. I was busy putting in full days, commuting and preparing for my teaching each day. I also knew that teaching in Sydney would be a short-term gig.

I was gaining valuable teaching experience, although I was discouraged when a lesson was observed by the Director of Studies who gave me rather harsh feedback. Since that experience, I have maintained that it is important when evaluating lessons to offer instructors positive and constructive tips for improvement. I concluded that this serves the practical goal of promoting better teaching.

I hung in at ACE for eight weeks. My time there taught me about the quality of teaching required. I learned first-hand the business imperative behind the organization's mission to create positive learning and socio-cultural experiences for international students. The lessons I learned were to stand me in good stead.

We returned to Calgary at the end of February 1988. A feeling of triumph and optimism hung over the city, which had just successfully hosted the Winter Olympics. It was contagious. I was hired to teach ESL part-time at Mount Royal College (now Mount Royal University). There was no pressure to perform under constant scrutiny as there had been at the Australian College of English. Highly motivated by my students, I was happy to share my lesson ideas and found that most other teachers reciprocated.

However, a great source of tension in the staffroom was photocopying. Photocopying to language teachers can be like a drug, even in the digital age. Mount Royal had instituted a policy limiting teachers to 100 pages a week onsite, enough for one printed page per day for each student in our classes. If we sent requests through the inter-campus courier at least three days in advance, we could get almost unlimited numbers of copies printed off at the main campus. This required more pre-planning than most teachers were prepared for in their busy lives.

Our manager announced that he was going to meet with each teacher and follow that up with lesson observations. Most of my colleagues were feisty. Photocopying was going to be the flashpoint. Comments floated around the staffroom promoting the idea that "we're each going to tell him that this photocopying limit is just not right."

I was scheduled to meet the manager last. When I walked into the meeting, his head was down. He looked exhausted after dealing with the insistent demands of my teacher colleagues. After we made our introductions, he said flatly, "So what do you want to talk about?"

I replied, "I don't want to talk about photocopying."

He sat up straight, smiled and said, "Well that's a relief."

We hit it off and had a good conversation about the students, approaches to lessons, and classroom management. A week or so later he observed my lesson and afterwards shared his affirming feedback.

My students had immigrated from many different countries. I learned a lesson about not making assumptions from a class list, which I perused before my first lesson. I saw that there was one student from Iran and another from Iraq. This was at the time when the war between those two countries had been going on for eight years.

"Would these guys get on?" I wondered.

The first class showed that my anxieties about this had been for naught. The two students had met two years earlier on a flight from West Germany (several years before the reunification of Germany) to Calgary, after they had each been accepted as refugee claimants to Canada. On the flight, they recognized that they were leaving Iran and Iraq respectively for the same reason, which was to find a better life. They had lost touch after they settled in Calgary, so meeting in class was like a brotherly reunion. They sat together in class each day, smiling and comfortable in each other's company.

I supplemented classroom activities with a field trip to the Glenbow Museum, where we saw an itinerant dentist's drill, which was operated by a foot pedal.

"In the Soviet Union where I am from," smiled Natasha enigmatically, "we still use this."

She had been a nuclear physicist and years later, when Global Village Calgary opened, I sometimes ran into Natasha, who had taken a good job in the oil and gas sector. She kindly told me how helpful the class had been for her. Language teachers, like instructors and professors everywhere, live for these moments.

There was also Denis, a Canadian from Quebec. One day he offered to help me outside of class. He noticed that I had residues of brown paint on my fingers. When I told him I was staining my fence at home, he offered to help if he could practise his English.

Meeting Denis was part of my coming to understand perspectives from other Canadians. He gave me an insight into how many from "La Belle Province" do not seem bothered by the conundrum of being from a distinct society that is also part of Canada. I have always seen it as a cool thing that Canada has two official languages, which laid a foundation for cultural pluralism.

The cultural mix of students in my class generally worked well. This provided a springboard for discussion of many topics. In the context of improving their English, the students explored subjects and customs from their own countries in relation to their lives in Canada.

There were the occasional frustrations with my class as well. I got annoyed one day with the consistent lateness of the Latin Americans in the class.

"Now look here," I said directly, "I'm here every day, all ready to start class at 9 a.m. So are most of your classmates. It's disruptive for the rest of us when you come in five, ten, even fifteen minutes late."

Then I was delayed one cold morning getting to work. The penny dropped! That morning it became clear to me that, for students with families, getting kids to daycare and to school meant that it was often difficult to get to class on time.

As well as teaching ESL in the mornings, I taught evening classes for adult immigrants for both Mount Royal College and the Calgary Board of Education. I also volunteered for the position of chair of the Calgary local branch of the Alberta Teachers of ESL (ATESL). Through ATESL, I helped with the annual conferences and initiatives like best practices. By June 1989 I was ready for the next chapter.

TIPS

If you are a teacher:

- Engage in staffroom causes that serve the interests of students, colleagues and your career
- Work constructively with teachers, administrative staff and students no matter what your role is in a language program
- Remember that adult students have many life concerns as the background soundtrack to their studies
- Ensure that all students feel accepted and validated in the community of the classroom
- Search for variety in your teaching throughout your career, including with different age and proficiency levels and with diverse learning programs
- Seek insights and improve your teaching skills constantly

A university Language Program

In June 1989 I saw an advertisement in the career section of the *Calgary Herald* for a coordinator of the English Language Centre at the University in Lethbridge, 210 kilometres south of Calgary. Two departments were being amalgamated into one with the ESL[3] Program being combined with the Writing Centre, which managed the Alberta Universities Writing Competence Test.

I sent in my application for the position. I longed for the security of a full-time job. A month passed and my hopes faded. Then, out of the blue, I received a phone call from the Secretary for the Dean of Student Affairs. Would I be available for an interview at the University of Lethbridge?

I met the charismatic Dean plus the Head of Human Resources, the Assistant Registrar and a faculty member from the School of English. This was an engaging committee and we had a very positive conversation. They liked that I was involved in ATESL[4] and my range of teaching experience. They were especially interested in the fact that I had been involved in private sector ESL for a time in Australia. It became clear that the Dean had a specific business model in mind for the new English Language Centre.

After answering all the committee's questions, the Dean asked if I had any comments or questions.

I asked, "What's happening with the current incumbents at the head of each of the two departments which are being combined?"

The Dean replied, "Well, the Writing Centre Coordinator is going home to the United States. The Head of ESL wants to stay on."

---

3   English as a Second Language (ESL)
4   Alberta Teachers of English as a Second Language (ATESL)

The Dean referred obliquely to others who had been interviewed and said that I was the last of four candidates. I was stunned when, at the end of the meeting, I was offered the position. I said that I would get back to them the next day, although in my mind I was certain I would accept their offer. On the drive back to Calgary, my thoughts bubbled away with all the implications of this career opportunity.

Cathie also knew that I had to take the job. Thus we started another period of transition, relocating our family from Calgary to Lethbridge. Cathie, who had been working in Calgary with the Technical Resource Centre (one of the early innovators of helping people with disabilities access computers), was able to find work in Lethbridge with community health projects.

As someone once told me, "Living in Lethbridge is like living in a hair dryer, with the settings on high or low at different times of the seasons."

It was a genuinely nice city to live in, especially when the wind did not blow. When we could, we cycled in Lethbridge and the surrounding river valleys with our friends Lisa and Fred.

I found my role at the University of Lethbridge challenging. I had to take a hard look at how the classes were being taught and if the ESL program was effective in meeting the requirements of the international students. As suspected, the previous coordinator resisted the transition to a new business model.

In my opinion, the program was constrained in several ways. First, teaching for the TOEFL (Test of English as a Foreign Language) was ineffective. At the time, TOEFL was based very much on grammatical structures but not on how language is used in a variety of contexts. Most of the students, who were mainly from Hong Kong, did not even need to take the TOEFL to meet English Language Proficiency. The University of Lethbridge was one of the first institutions in Canada to adopt its own pathway program. Thus, the English Language Centre (ELC) had a clear charter to prepare students to meet the English requirements for degree studies.

Within the small department of three ESL instructors, I asked questions about the preferred way of doing things. At the time, there were about 50 students in the ESL program. I could see potential for that to increase to over 100 students.

Classes were focussed on academic writing for the TOEFL. The teachers complained vociferously about the amount of marking. When I reviewed student papers after they had been marked, I found that they were heavily covered in teachers' red ink.

In a meeting with teachers, I wondered aloud if the students took heed in correcting errors and if they completed more than one draft of their writing assignments. My colleagues shook their heads and collectively sighed, "Not usually."

"You see, the thing is that you seem to be working harder on the student essays than they are," I said.

I advised that the teachers could reduce their marking time and be more effective by giving students focussed feedback. Research on writing suggested that teachers and students target specific skills rather than the totality of errors. There was also strong evidence supporting the idea that students' writing improves with their attending to corrections made to first, second or more drafts. In teachers' meetings, we discussed how students could be graded partly on how they improved their writing through engagement in a process. Teachers began to buy into these approaches when they saw that the onus for improvement would be on students working with teachers, rather than on teachers merely correcting errors.

In the fall of 1989, my ELC teaching colleagues began to utilize computer-assisted language learning as one of their instructional tools. By saving their drafts on the 3.5-inch floppy discs of that era, students could then go back and work on other drafts. They also improved their keyboarding skills, which were going to be important as the personal computer came to the fore in our lives. These were early days in the adoption of technology for language learning. At the University of Lethbridge, we started using email in

1992 but our use of the Internet did not take off until 1995. Even then, it was a few years before we moved beyond the tedious dial-up for connecting. Wireless technology was a thing of the future.

I had to battle for class computer time in the only lab of the Modern Languages Department at the University of Lethbridge. It was obvious that ESL as a non-credit program was marginalized in this university setting. Faculty members who taught credit courses thought they had precedence, mainly because they did. The English Language Centre was assigned classroom space only after classrooms for credit courses had been assigned at the beginning of each semester. Our classes were sometimes in windowless rooms in the far reaches of the campus, which felt like the Siberian outskirts in the winter months. Furthermore, it was not unknown for faculty to turn up early for their classes and expect ESL teachers to vacate a classroom even when our allotted time was not up.

A winter chill settled on Lethbridge and by Christmas Eve, 1989 it was 35^5 below. I was trying to figure out how many classes to run for the new January semester. As my colleagues partied in the open space of Student Affairs and the Christmas cheeriness became louder, a group of five Mexican students came to see me about starting classes at the beginning of the new year. They were frozen, having walked in unaccustomed temperatures to find me.

These registrations were a godsend. The day before, I had interviewed a new potential teacher, Nancy, who had a very positive outlook and great ESL teaching credentials. Now I was going to be able to add one more class and hire her. Giving her the news just before Christmas warmed the spirit. Nancy was to have a powerfully positive impact teaching at University of Lethbridge for ten years and later worked with me at both Global Village Calgary and GV Victoria.

During this cold Canadian winter, we decided that the cost of tuition had been undervalued. We increased our fees from $850 to

---

5   Minus 35 degrees Celsius

$1140, both arbitrary figures, but the latter was more in line with what we saw other Canadian universities charging for 14 weeks of 25 hours of instruction per week. The Dean and I were applying the theory that if we built up the ESL program, more international students would come to the University of Lethbridge. We also knew that if we charged more for ESL courses, students would expect higher quality instruction and better personal results.

I tried to come up with marketing strategies to attract more international students to the ESL program. At the time, the university did not work with agents, who are usually based in non-English-speaking countries and send students on a commission basis (often as an extension of their travel businesses). Marketing ESL at the University of Lethbridge very much depended on word of mouth about the quality of what was happening in the classroom and whether the level of instruction assisted students in meeting their goals. At the University of Lethbridge, students in the ESL program wanted to be accepted into degree programs as quickly as possible. We wanted them to have the skills to be successful once they got there.

We workshopped approaches in classes. It was clear that students needed to become better at soft skills like time management, collaborating with other students and asking questions of their instructors. We strongly encouraged students, both in the ESL and Writing program, to arrange their thoughts productively in individual and group assignments and to be active in their learning generally. We promoted activities that prompted speaking up in class and accountability for each student in paired or group interactions with their classmates.

We explained to students that active engagement and not sitting back in class with an "entertain me" attitude served their interests in making progress. There was also a discernible student-as-client mentality. Some thought the fees that they paid entitled them to automatic graduation from the ESL program into university degrees. This, of course, was not the case.

At the same time, we wrestled with the aspirations and expectations of the international students. We found it hard to shift them to the ethos of a liberal arts education, where students are encouraged to be critical thinkers. Many international students have not been encouraged to think critically and to discuss or debate issues. We found them to be more comfortable with the model of teacher as the source of knowledge. In their formal education in their home countries, students often look to satisfy their teachers in class-based assignments, term papers and exams by regurgitating opinions that they think will make their teachers happy.

Overall, we were making progress in our work at the English Language Centre. The team of instructors understood our mandate. I made a habit of explaining some of the administrative challenges that most teachers could discern in the wider university context, while supporting their classroom focus.

However, one colleague, the previous ESL Coordinator and erstwhile instructor was having difficulty. If she had come to accept the changes, she had done so grudgingly. She decided to leave. Under other conditions, we may have worked well together. Putting those thoughts aside, I led with the optimism of a new season. I felt we had a team that was willing to pull in one direction.

With increasing student enrollment and a higher tuition base, the ELC witnessed a dramatic increase in revenue. This pleased the Dean. But we discovered that an intended one-time correctional increase in tuition was assumed by the university's senior administration to signal significant revenue increases every year. As a result, the ELC was expected to be a cash cow while it continued to increase and diversify the international student population. It seemed both onerous and short-sighted. Yet this was happening to other programs too, as the Alberta government adjusted its model for funding public education.

While all the changes were occurring in the ESL program, things were not standing still with our sister program, writing services. We developed the Writing for University non-credit course. This enabled international and Canadian students to work together on language skills required for academic writing. They often came to the program after underestimating the Alberta Universities Writing Competence Test (AUWCT). The AUWCT required students to write a 400-word essay of argument under supervised conditions with follow-up interviews available.

The Writing for University course allowed English Language Centre instructors to work on a more qualitative, process approach requiring students to polish their drafts of different types of essays every two weeks over the 12-week course. The writing side of the Centre, along with the ESL program, that had grown to over 100 students in the spring of 1990, kept me busy. Although most of my role was administrative, I taught the writing course twice a week. It kept me tuned in to the needs of both the students and the teachers.

I sought out faculty who were interested in helping University of Lethbridge students to write better. One professor in the Faculty of Education initiated a project called Writing Across the Curriculum. Many faculty members were frustrated by having to mark essays that had basic errors made by both Canadian-born and international students alike. The Education professor saw it as one of the instructors' responsibilities to help students improve their writing, but many faculty members did not. Their school of thought contended that students should already have the skills necessary to produce good term papers.

Working with interested faculty members and with the support of the Deans of the Faculties of Management and Student Affairs, we had sessions which encouraged interested faculty members to speak to their views on how writing in a liberal arts institution was important and to share strategies aimed at improving general standards.

These interdepartmental sessions were held throughout an academic year and were instructive in demonstrating the need to educate faculty, diplomatically of course, in what counted as good writing among international students. Some faculty gave disproportionately lower grades because of ESL student errors, like the omission of definite articles, that were trivial in the overall scheme of things. I pointed out that language acquisition research supported the hypothesis that these were elements of grammar that only came with long-term proficiency and growth in usage of English as a second language. I encouraged faculty to look at the strength of organization and the consistency of the presentation of ideas in student essays. These were key elements that our ESL and writing course instructors dealt with, along with helping students with the mechanical underpinnings of grammar, vocabulary and sentence structure.

Of course, as in any workplace setting, people in a university all have their agendas and priorities. Only a small minority of faculty engaged in the Writing Across the Curriculum project, but they represented a cross-section of disciplines on campus. The project created discussion and a better understanding of how to meet the aspirations of both students and faculty for student writing.

The University of Lethbridge in those days was housed almost exclusively in a huge rectangular building designed by Arthur Erickson[6], the famous Canadian architect. It sits nestled against steep coulees above the Oldman River. The campus was part of a stunning prairie landscape on the west side of Lethbridge, facing the city across the river. Lethbridge had a population of about 60,000 at the time.

As we expanded the size of both the ESL and writing programs, we were constantly on a quest for more classrooms and office space. Towards the end of the summer in 1990, all the different departments within Student Affairs moved up the hill on campus

---

6   University of Lethbridge, designed by Arthur Erickson with Geoffrey Massey (1968)

from their digs in the main Erickson Building to the new semi-spherical building, which looked like an expanded version of the Starship Enterprise.

Space for staff of the ELC had not been adequately planned. I now worked alongside four full-time teachers and two part-time instructors. We were spread out in cubicles, or "veal-fattening pens" as they were called, around the large Student Affairs open plan area. Students had good access to our reception area, just inside the main doors of Student Affairs. However, students had to follow a maze around the cubicles to meet with teachers.

I convinced the Dean that we needed a consolidated area for our staff, so a room large enough for four or five teachers was conjured out of some empty space in the basement of the "Enterprise". It was not ideal, but it was functional and allowed teachers to collaborate. I found myself in a decent office on the periphery of the first floor of the building, tucked away next to the counsellors' offices, and within walking distance of the Dean's office.

By the summer of 1994, five years in Lethbridge had passed. Cathie had a position with the Regional Centre for Health Promotion and Community Studies. Having completed her master's degree in Community Health Sciences in 1993, she was looking at doing a PhD, as I was. I was also frustrated with the growing marginalization of the English Language Centre within the university environment.

Cathie was pregnant with our long-awaited second child. We set our sights on moving to Calgary at the end of August 1995, as Cathie was accepted at the University of Calgary to study for a PhD and I was admitted to the PhD program in education.

It was to be our last year in Lethbridge. The stress increased at the University of Lethbridge when the President mandated that every administrative department, that was not within a faculty, support all their "true costs" as "ancillary operations". The English Language Centre had been producing revenue for the university, but now I was asked for a business plan which would include covering the rent on campus spaces we occupied and other administrative overhead. The Centre had not absorbed such costs up to this point. It was apparent that senior decision-makers failed to recognize that we in the ELC were instrumental in helping international students enter degree programs and succeed. International students paid significantly higher tuition than domestic students, but universities in Alberta were scrambling to cut costs and raise in-house revenue in the light of provincial government funding cutbacks.

Word came down from the President's office that my department's comprehensive business plan would have to be completed by the beginning of March 1995. This was right at the time when our baby was due. The President granted a one-week extension for me to hand in my business plan.

March 2, 1995 was a snowy, typical late-winter day in keeping with the Alberta-weather saying about March "in like a lion and out like a lamb." David James was born around 11 a.m. This was a wonderful and life-affirming event in our family.

With a sense of relief in removing the albatross from around my neck, I handed in the business plan. We resolved to put our house on the market and move by the beginning of the fall semester to Calgary to begin PhD programs. Within a few months, I informed others that I was leaving the English Language Centre at the University of Lethbridge.

We had a brief holiday in Waterton Lakes National Park, about 130 kilometres southwest of Lethbridge, nestled in a pristine setting in the Canadian Rockies. We have a picture of the boys at the gravesite of John George Kootenai Brown, an early explorer and settler in the area. It is a snapshot of our family at the time. John George, nine, is leaning on a fence while David, almost six months old, plays in the grass. The parents, Cathie and I, look young, tired and hopeful.

TIPS

If you are a teacher:

- Engage with your fellow instructors and administrative staff as a collaborative team member with positive comments

- Remind yourself of key program goals and the value of your work with students

- Recognize that your manager may bear the brunt of wider institutional pressures on your program

If you are a manager:

- Form a team of believers on your own staff and maintain a focus on promoting quality instruction

- Ensure that professional development and peer support are ongoing priorities

- Understand and prepare to challenge established mores in your department and/or the wider institutional setting

- Expect that a non-credit language program for international students may be marginalized in a post-secondary context

- Network with faculty and acquaint college or university decision-makers with the work of your program

- Prepare for constant change with a language program within a public sector institution

40   Easier Said Than Done

Japanese Student Exchange

In February 1991, the University of Lethbridge's Dean of Student Affairs paid me a visit. "How would you like to go to Japan on the Hokkaigakuen Student Exchange?"

The cultural exchange program enabled faculty and students from the respective universities to go back and forth between Lethbridge and Hokkaido (the northern island of Japan) as part of the Alberta-Hokkaido twinning agreement. I said yes! Then, I travelled with fifteen University of Lethbridge students and one other faculty member, from late May into June.

The few days we had in Kyoto, before immersing ourselves in the official study part of the program in Hokkaido, included trips to the iconic temples and gardens. A day trip to Hiroshima was incredibly moving. We visited the site of the bombed-out bell tower and surrounding areas, as well as the museum which contained the infamous broken watch that was frozen in time at the exact moment when the bomb impacted, among many poignant artifacts. We were taken to the Hiroshima Gardens, a symbol of the resurrection of the city and beauty in the face of overwhelming tragedy and suffering. As the student group and I returned by bus and bullet train to Kyoto, not a word was spoken. We were all lost in contemplation.

Being in Japan gave me fascinating insights into its culture and history. The Japanese people I met retained a dignity and appreciation of beauty amidst their hard-working, everyday routines.

But I had to keep my wits about me with our group of Canadian students. On the night before leaving Kyoto, one student drank so much that she gave herself alcohol poisoning. We spent an anxious and sleepless night as she slept it off. The next morning, the other faculty member wanted to send her back home. I advocated for her to stay, not only to give her a second chance, but because it was going to be extremely hard to explain to our hosts if we turned up one student short.

We flew to Sapporo, where the other faculty member gathered the group together in the midst of Japanese commuters and read the riot act to the students. Even after just a few days in their country, I could feel the quietude of the Japanese among all the hustle and bustle. It was embarrassing to be standing in the airport as *gaijin* (foreigners), with one person berating the rest of the group.

After those initial hiccups though, everything went swimmingly. We flew to the northeast of Hokkaido for the first part of the Hokkaigakuen program in the small city of Kitami. We were there for ten days. I stayed on campus, which was in a peaceful rural setting, while the students were accommodated by host families in nearby homes.

In Kitami we went to classes where we learned some rudimentary Japanese plus more about Japanese history and culture. I became friendly with one professor, Shinzo and his wife, Cheiko. Over supper at their home in Kitami, Shinzo expanded on the topic of high- and low-context cultures. This was the subject of the lecture he had given us that day. His point was that Japan is a high-context culture, where people are very attuned to the nuances of each situation, whereas in Western countries, things were less nuanced and less formal in most settings.

Japanese formality was replete with overtones, some of which we in the Lethbridge group found hilarious. There was a lot of symbolism built into interactions in Japan. I committed my share of innocent faux pas. For example, when I was invited to supper at Shinzo's and Chieko's home, I picked up some flowers to thank them for hosting me. Shinzo laughed and politely pointed out that the flowers I had picked were for grieving relatives.

Our time as Westerners in Japan was filled with negotiations around the unfamiliar. I was unwittingly caught out repeatedly. Another incident happened at a hotel. Unbeknownst to a *gaijin* like me, the Japanese hotel where we stayed in Sounkyo Gorge on our way to Sapporo reversed the use by men and women of the hot baths called *onsens*. They changed the schedule between Saturday night and Sunday morning. This was later explained to me, based on the very Japanese logic, that equalizing the use of the facilities by the heavier men and the lighter women would allow for equal wear and tear on the floor tiles.

Just after waking up in a Sunday morning fog, I inadvertently walked into the women's area. The wide-eyed, relaxed elderly ladies soaking in the water were unfazed. The jokester of the group motioned for me to come over, saying something in Japanese as she flexed an arm muscle. This was the universal signal for "Come on over and get in the water with us, big strong man."

Her friends laughed. I smilingly demurred, apologized and beat a hasty retreat.

I was relieved to get back to Lethbridge after four weeks away. Although it had been an incredible experience to go to Japan, it was very taxing to be apart from my family and to navigate the language and customs of Japan. The trip increased my empathy for international students and the challenges they face when they leave their countries. It felt great to be back home, like a fish swimming in the right water again.

In 1993 I travelled to Japan again on the student exchange. The trip proceeded along a similar trajectory as two years before. This trip was extended to five weeks because I had an additional journey to Yamanashi Eiwa High School in the shadow of Mount Fuji. (This extra time away made it even harder for our family. I missed Cathie and John George terribly.) The visit to the girls' school was a way of cementing the exchange program. Starting in 1991, Yamanashi Eiwa sent thirty students and two staff each summer for three weeks to the program at the University of Lethbridge. This program continued for years.

When the Hokkaigakuen students made their reciprocal visits to Lethbridge in 1990, 1992 and 1994, the English Language Centre organized classes and assisted with activities, excursions and finding volunteer host families among the university community. We worked hard to make the program successful.

Overall, the exchange experiences had a profound effect on many lives. Lethbridge and the surrounding area of southern Alberta has a strong Japanese heritage. Five of the fifteen students on each of the 1991 and 1993 Japan trips were second- or third-generation Japanese Canadians. Many of the Lethbridge students went back to work as English teachers in Japan. Two students, who met on the 1991 exchange, married. One student from the 1993 trip worked in Obihiro in Hokkaido for several years and met his Japanese wife there. We kept in touch and he became an interim on-site manager at Global Village Victoria for a short time in 2005.

I learned many lessons about cultural interactions and about myself from my time in Japan. I learned that I had to dig deep for patience and humility when the language and customs of Japan threatened to overwhelm me. I gained insight into the wrenching feelings of homesickness that can almost paralyze people when they are far away from their comfort zones. The student exchange trips to Japan as well as the ones we hosted in Lethbridge, also opened my eyes to all the moving parts in the administration of an international study program and the flexibility needed by program participants, whether you are the hosts or the hosted.

TIPS

If you are a teacher or an administrative staff member:

- Foster opportunities to travel and interact with people across cultures
- Be prepared to learn new lessons about yourself and others
- Nurture your own career by being open to new experiences such as international exchanges

If you are a manager:

- All the above, plus
- Ask about the breadth of experience of potential hires

School Start-up

The first day that Global Village Calgary opened for classes, dawned sunny and frigid, with a temperature of minus 35° Celsius, a classic prairie winter day. It was January 15, 1996. As Cathie drove me up to Gulf Canada Square, the high-rise office tower that housed the school, we saw a young man with bright red snow boots. He was picking his way precariously along the ridge of a metre-high snowbank beside Ninth Avenue. He looked like he was trekking across an alien arctic environment. "Is he one of your students?" Cathie asked.

Smiling, I replied, "I'm pretty sure he is."

Our small staff of three administrative staff and three teachers met the students. We behaved as if we had been operating as a school for years. On that first day, the students, who were all adults, were tested for their English levels, given some orientation (in which the most important details were how to dress and stay warm in Calgary), and arranged into three classes.

Our enrollment grew quickly. Two months before the Calgary school opened, the GV Managing Director and the Marketing Manager in Vancouver, were very concerned at the low registration rate and dropped the tuition for the whole year of 1996 by 30 percent. What this major discount meant was that we were constantly under pressure with a rapidly expanding student body and program with a low revenue base.

By March 1996, we had 80 students and were able to move from the fourth to the ninth floor of Gulf Canada Square, where we expanded into nine classrooms. We also had an option on an adjoining space for another seven classrooms. Altogether, this made a total space of about 10,000 square feet (930 square metres).

The relocation resulted in more frantic and intensive work on weekends as well as long days and nights at the school, setting up once again. One time, Lynn, the Homestay Coordinator and Assistant Director, and I were putting up whiteboards. I was drilling and he was holding the boards in place. While I operated the drill, Lynn suddenly shifted position to hold the board in place so that his head was just below where I was making holes in the wall.

"Look, Lynn," I joked, "I appreciate your faith in my steady hand, but my handyman skills are not that great. If I slip up, you're going to get a lobotomy and I'm going to end up doing homestay on my own!"

Such moments of hilarity broke the stress. Lynn's positive outlook helped set the tone for staff and students. At different times, often even on the same day, our small, engaged staff was both energized and exhausted by the growth of the enterprise. We were registering more students and hiring more teachers.

Working with the GV Marketing Manager, we tried to attract more students from a variety of countries. Most of the student population in our first months was Korean. This proved a solid basis for GV Calgary's enrollment. Our timing with attracting students from Korea was excellent. Koreans were just starting to travel in greater numbers as international students. Global Village Calgary rode this wave right through to 2020, with our Korean students being the number one nationality represented in the school.

The cities of Calgary and Seoul were linked by the fact that each had hosted Olympic Games. Consequently, South Koreans knew about Calgary. We offered a less expensive location for language study than the bigger cities. Throughout the subsequent years, international recognition of Calgary grew. However, when we were first setting up, many around the world had not heard of our city. Or, if they had, they may have thought that we lived in igloos in the frozen north.

The influx of Korean students led to the necessity for some of them to receive cultural competence training. Most Korean male students came to us straight from military service in Korea and had rarely travelled to a western country previously. We came up against the negative attitude of a few students who did not take kindly to classes directed by female teachers. Lynn initiated diplomatic conversations with those paternalistic students to reset their orientations. He also advised other staff members as well as host families about how to communicate with students about aspects of Canadian culture.

As a group, the Korean students were known to test the limits of our tolerance. One of the outcomes of the quick growth of the student population was that some students who had been with us since the first day of classes, including our first registered student, In Sook Kim, started to complain. They had enjoyed being part of our start-up student population of 27 students. Now they had to adapt to a larger community of students. Also, Global Village Calgary was becoming less like what they were used to back home, where they studied in classes with all Korean classmates. Plus, they had to wait longer for their turns at table tennis in the student lounge.

Things came to a head when we had a visiting delegation of Mexican agents. I caught wind of a group of Koreans in the student lounge orchestrating a protest against the growing number of students. They were one step away from making banners and headbands with slogans, which are the hallmarks of protest marches in Asia.

While Lynn corralled the Mexican visitors in a distant part of the school, I strode into the student lounge and appealed to In Sook Kim, the ringleader, to wrap up the demonstration. I had had a good rapport with him since the first day the school opened. But now he turned on me, emboldened by about twenty comrades-in-arms.

He began, "In South Korea, we have history of student protest."

"I'm going to stop you right there, In Sook," I interrupted. "Because you are not in South Korea. You are in Canada now."

"But we want change. There are too many students."

I thought briefly about all the work that we had done to get this far. Of course, the whole business concept depended on a reasonably sufficient volume of students to offset our increasing expenses. This was especially significant in that first year as all students were paying under market value for their programs, and the agents were already asking for higher commissions.

I said, "Excuse me, but you don't get to decide how many students we have in the school. That's a decision for administration. Besides, learning English is better with students from other countries," I added, trying to throw him off his focus on the number of students.

He glowered at me, while the rest of the students shifted uncomfortably. I sensed that most of them were not really committed to the protest movement. Knowing that the Mexican agents would soon be moving through the school, and wanting to avoid a public standoff, I resorted to highlighting a different irritant.

It was our "English only" policy. The idea is that students use English not only in class time, but also at all other times while they are in the school. The theory is that if students practise English even while they are outside classes in the school location, they should improve. I pointed out the intent of the policy and that many of the Korean students had not been using English in the school. This shifted the focus. There was another awkward silence.

I added, "It's the end of the day, so I'm going to ask you all to go home and have a think about learning English and what would help you make the most of your time here in Calgary. Most students are here because they want a different experience to what they have back home. Each of you is going to have to change your thinking and accept that there will be more students from other countries in the school. That's how you will really benefit from your study experience in Canada." The protestors drifted away.

It had turned into a bit of a speech, but I had managed to keep my tone even. I remember feeling surprised at my passion about what I was saying. I am not sure that all or even most of the students took on board what I had said. But there it was. There is always a risk of alienating students or staff when one points out a few salient facts or shares opinions. Still, it felt therapeutic for me. I had vented some of my stress through an impromptu statement that crystalized what Global Village Calgary was about.

Lynn entered the lounge. "That was close," we silently communicated. The tour with the friendly Mexican agents continued uninterrupted.

There were many priorities in the start-up of Global Village Calgary. In developing the business, we needed to build trust, add depth to our programs, create international diversity in the student population, deal with cultural differences in the expectations of the students and host families, and try to maintain good relations with our neighbours in the building.

In addition to the day-to-day issues that I attended to as manager of the school, I had to navigate Calgary's way through the centralized GV Vancouver management system. We were finding that the streamlining of services did offer economies of scale but also opened the door to unforeseen local problems and related stress.

For example, the finances for GV Calgary were controlled on the west coast by GV Vancouver. Because they were sent from Vancouver, the cheques for host families were frequently delayed. This was in the days before the ease of online money transfers. The host families would call us, impatiently expecting us to solve the problem. We discovered that our IT[7] support was also not at the level we needed. We relied on a staff member at GV Vancouver, where his work at the burgeoning west coast school was his priority. He had little time or energy left to devote to our concerns.

On March 31, 1996 Lynn and I flew to Vancouver for a day of meetings. It had been a long Calgary winter and it still was not over. As we took off, we looked out from the plane at the sun shining on

---

7   Information Technology (IT)

deep layers of snow, lying like a shroud over the city. It was minus 20° Celsius. Vancouver, though, was in a different season and it felt like we were in a different country when we arrived. Spring had sprung. Flowers and bushes were budding. The sun reflected off the nearby mountains on one of those pristine days that Vancouver can deliver.

We did not get to enjoy the beautiful weather outside, however. We spent the day, along with west-coast staffers, in discussions led by the GV Managing Director. His purpose was to impress upon us the benefits of the centralized administrative model. Touching down in Calgary at the end of another long day, the thermometer had not shifted from minus 20.

The long winter was ending. However, something had to give. I had embraced the opportunity, that had been presented by the GV Vancouver board members, to get in on the ground floor for Global Village Calgary. Before we left Lethbridge, Cathie and I agreed that I would take on the start-up of a new school and a PhD program, at least initially, and see where the adventure would lead.

By April, I had completed the courses for a PhD in Education (but still needed to complete candidacy and a dissertation) while Cathie also did her course work for her PhD. We arranged our schedules so that either Cathie or myself would be coming in the door while the other was going to classes or, often in my case, from another long day downtown.

It just was not sustainable for both of us to be doing PhDs. I was still very much engaged in all the details of a start-up business, often working 60 hours a week downtown as well as taking a full university course load. As much as I wanted to pursue an academic life, it was daunting to think of at least two more years of plugging away at a PhD. Meanwhile, the workload and stresses at GV Calgary showed no signs of abating. At the end of the winter semester, I put my PhD on hold, while in truth I recognized that I was not likely ever to complete it. I had second thoughts for a couple of years but my initial sense of the situation proved true.

My academic course work and interests led me into researching the importance of writing as a language learning skill and how the language learning process went better for students who adopted tolerance for ambiguity as a strategy. This line of enquiry gave credence to encouraging students not to get preoccupied with mastery of every component of the target language. The thinking suggested that if students could go with the flow of being immersed in a new language, they would be better served than if they were focussed on every grammatical or idiomatic nuance. I concluded that in language learning and teaching, as in life, obsession with the parts, rather than contemplating the whole, often leads to feeling overwhelmed.

In the flash of a light-bulb moment, during this period of personal and professional upheaval, I realized that tolerance for ambiguity could be applied to my management approach. I was dealing with an expanding, complex business which was populated by many difficult characters and situations. A pragmatic approach did not entail a lack of attention to detail, an aspect that I saw as one of my skills. However, I had to give my head a shake if I became obsessed with things or strove for perfection. In the dynamic of the day-to-day work, and as a coping mechanism, I decided to adopt tolerance for ambiguity as a personal creed without compromising my values.

Along with our colleagues at other Global Village schools in Hawaii, Toronto and Vancouver, we were concerned with the practical applications of co-funding and working with GV Marketing. We discovered, for instance, that we needed to adapt our price point for tuition and commissions so that we could enroll students from a diversity of countries.

We were also ensuring that values such as having an advanced duty of care for students was built into the culture of the GV schools. We needed teachers and administrative staff to be on board with high standards of professionalism. Our goals may have been obvious to ourselves as managers, but we wanted all staff to be clear. We found it necessary to explicate the expectation in meetings, both with staff as a whole and with individuals, that we were serious about functioning as a team and setting and maintaining a positive atmosphere in each location.

Several more months passed. By July at GV Calgary, we were bursting at the seams with 200 students. The one photocopier broke down regularly from overuse. The copier, which was near my office, often had a forlorn, beaten-up look about it after the morning flurry of activity. I noticed it sitting there seemingly exhausted with its lid up, like a vehicle with its hood propped open by the side of a highway. Often the technician would have his head in the machine, completing the image of the copier as an untrustworthy car, constantly being tended to by a mechanic. I projected a certain empathy onto that overworked copier.

We now had 16 classrooms including a computer lab. I recall that we moved the table tennis out of the relatively small student lounge, where people had been constantly ducking out of the way of the over-exuberant players. Students could now play table tennis in a spare classroom tucked away from others. We had to ask the students to tone down their play, which proceeded among the male students at Olympic-style ferocity.

The Korean students were coming around, though. They were respectful when we asked them not to dive headlong into the walls when making their shots, although the wear and tear on the room showed evidence of their rambunctious play when we were not looking. At other times, they slowed their pace and played doubles with some members of staff and female students in the school.

Increasingly, the Korean students were accepting and enjoying having students from other countries in their classes. It was a delicate balance, though, as some Korean students and their agents complained that there were "too many Koreans", even as they secretly enjoyed a strong Korean flavour at GV Calgary. That was also a literal concept as the smell of kimchi, a favourite Korean food, wafted from the student lounge during lunch breaks.

During our period of intense, rapid growth and the plethora of challenges in the early years of GV Calgary, we sought to get on well with our neighbours in the building. Our language school was an anomaly among the business tenants in Gulf Canada Square. There were quite a few oil and gas companies and others in the suit-and-tie brigade, like merchant bankers, who were located on the same floor as our school. They had to share the same washrooms with our students, which was a point of conflict. We also found allies such as the dentist down the hallway. I made it a priority to communicate with the building manager for Gulf Canada Square.

Our students were mainly adults over 18, but we also had quite a few students aged 16 and 17 years. When students got up to high jinks, other tenants in the building frowned upon us. Sometimes younger students liked to live on the edge. One student took this quite literally.

There was a main pedestrian thoroughfare, up the escalator from the expansive, well-appointed lobby of Gulf Canada Square. Next to the convenience shop run by the long-suffering but friendly Basil, there was an atrium garden. I received a call from the building manager telling me that one of our students had tried, like a trapeze artist, to walk across a narrow timber beam that separated two sections of this indoor garden.

Unfortunately, the student had lost his balance and fallen in. When I arrived, he was half covered in mud. I quickly assured the building manager that we would tell our students to refrain from traipsing across the garden, something that most people would find intuitively obvious! When I turned to head back upstairs, the student started following me, as if he was going back to class.

"No, no, you're done for the day. You can't go back into class like that," I quietly admonished as clumps of mud, which had congealed on the student's sodden clothes, started to fall off as he shuffled along. He and I were also receiving quizzical looks from folks in their business attire.

On another occasion, on a cold November day, GV Calgary received the attention of the whole of Gulf Canada Square in an altogether unwelcome way. One of our students, for a lark, pushed the fire alarm on our floor. Before we could call the emergency number to cancel the call, alarms were ringing throughout the whole building. A full-scale evacuation was underway.

An armada of firetrucks turned up with their sirens wailing and echoing throughout the heart of Calgary. The core of downtown Calgary came to a standstill with the piercing sirens providing the soundtrack to the general pandemonium. At least a thousand people emptied out of the twenty-story building and huddled outside for an hour in minus 20° Celsius. Soon, word spread that the alarm had been sounded on the ninth floor "where that international school is".

After the false alarm had been investigated and the good people of Gulf Canada Square had been allowed to return to their work, I did not have long to contemplate the fallout. The implications of the interruption to all the businesses and the resources that had been utilized by the Calgary Fire Department were enormous. The fire chief was angrily pacing up and down on the spot when I returned to the ninth floor.

"All right," he said. "This is the deal. We're going to fine your business $500."

This seemed a comparatively light sentence in view of the scope of the disruption. I could not even imagine a possible dollar figure for the loss of productivity for at least an hour of all the people in Gulf Canada Square businesses. Clearly, we were marked down as a tenant whose lease would not be renewed in the long term. But we were fortunate that there were minimal immediate negative repercussions from other tenants.

The building manager needed little persuasion to arrange to cover the small fire alarm pull switches with locked glass covers (which could be broken in an emergency, courtesy of small hammers hung on short, attached chains) so that they would not be as accessible to anyone who had a future brain cramp. We also included fire safety in our orientations for new students. There were no future mishaps with the fire alarms in Gulf Canada Square, although we lived on tenterhooks for a long time afterwards.

The reputation of Global Village Calgary was certainly not enhanced by the fire-alarm and garden-mud-walker incidents. We were often held responsible for the behaviour of our students. Both Lynn and I, as senior managers, wrestled with the dynamics of just how far we could be held accountable for people's actions, over which we clearly had no control. It came along with the territory of managing the activities and relationships within the business that was still finding its stride.

We had anticipated many challenges in the start-up years of Global Village Calgary but sometimes we were thrown off balance by many we had not expected. In retrospect, it seems that managers of start-up businesses seem to play an advanced form of Whac-A-Mole, the arcade game,[8] where you need to keep tamping down the multiple pieces that keep popping up, often simultaneously. Especially in the early years of GV Calgary, we needed to keep our eyes on the whole board and have quick reflexes. Rather than dealing with problems in a piecemeal fashion, we hoped to come up with long-lasting and effective solutions that would help us survive and flourish as a business.

---

8   Whac-A-Mole, a popular arcade game

TIPS

If you are a teacher:

- Focus on the people, such as personalities in the classroom, and not the copier machine
- Develop personal tolerance for ambiguity as an aspect of your professional growth
- Hold onto key values and let those guide you when times are tough
- Maintain a sense of humour

If you are a manager:

- All the above, and the following
- Clarify priorities in developing the business
- Ensure that you as a manager and your staff take a step back regularly to review priorities
- Consider how to deal with aberrant and non-malicious behaviour of students
- Be clear on your decision-making parameters if you are part of a group of schools or larger institution
- Develop tolerance for changes in the institution and if you are part of a group of schools

Adult Homestay

Working in the homestay department of a language school is not for the faint of heart. Finding host families was one of the first tasks we had in setting up a new school and Lynn, our Homestay Coordinator and Assistant School Director, had embraced the project. In the first four years of Global Village Calgary (in the second half of the 1990s), he had his hands full with recruiting families, dealing with student issues and attempting to keep the entire program and its participants on an even keel.

Fortunately, Lynn is a very clear-thinking communicator who had a mission to make the homestay experience for GV Calgary a positive component of the immersion experience for international students. He put together compelling messages for recruiting host families and built working relationships with them. Most hosts were motivated to be part of intercultural connections that went beyond the question of remuneration, which was also an issue to be navigated.

The influence of host families in accepting international students as part of their families, even for a brief time, can never be overvalued. Some host families decided in a brief time that the program was not for them. A few extremely dedicated stalwarts worked as hosts for more than 20 years with the school. Understandably, some host families needed periodic respites from hosting students.

When hosted by families, some students have their own issues or create problems. Those who act out are often sowing their wild oats. Many view their period of being an international student as an opportunity to not only learn English but also to cut loose, knowing that the years ahead back in their own countries will be career oriented. GV Calgary's host families, in general, understood the need to be flexible and tried to engage with students and include them in their family life.

Some students, though, caused their hosts concern. One weekend, when I was looking after the emergency homestay phone, I relayed one cryptic message to Lynn after a host mother called me, out of breath, to say, "Jorg has come home."

"Good," said Lynn, "I was wondering about him."

Jorg was away from his home country, Switzerland, for the first time and made the most of the Calgary Stampede festivities. He had not come home for three nights, nor was he sighted in class during that time. Students sometimes enjoyed the spirit of the Stampede a little too much. This was the time of the year in Calgary when the bar, pardon the pun, was already set low for people to be enjoying alcohol and having a good time. Once, one of our students had been witnessed walking along the middle of the tracks of the downtown light rail transit in Calgary's early morning light after a big night out during a Stampede heatwave.

It is the nature of homestay business for roiling intrigues to continue with a small proportion of students and their hosts. At GV Calgary we learned quickly that all managers in a language program, especially those with responsibilities in the homestay area, needed to prioritize issues. Homestay staff also required awareness and skills to deal with students who experienced homesickness, culture shock and anxiety. Conflict resolution skills were also necessary.

As the executive manager, I abhorred attempts to drag me into petty issues, such as one time when a student complained to me about the colour of the bath towels in a homestay. I tried to preserve energy to engage and be sharp when issues started to list towards possible legal problems or when people's safety might be compromised.

Once, a host father locked a student out of the home when she did not come home by 10 p.m. She was on a school activity attending a Calgary Flames National Hockey League (NHL) game that went into overtime. This incident could have been deadly serious as it was a cold night with the temperature well below zero (Celsius).

Luckily, the student knew another of our students staying nearby and her host family let the cold student in to stay for the night. The host father, who locked her out, seemed like a throwback to the "my house, my rules, no matter what" line of uncompromising thinking. It was better just to part ways. We learned to ask more questions of potential families and to trust our instincts, especially when GV Calgary staff did the home visits before approving homestays to accept our students.

We occasionally faced issues that could have become serious legal problems without strategic interventions. The school's receptionist would sometimes tell me that a host family member wanted to speak to me. In one of the first years of the school, a host mother was barely making sense as she almost hyperventilated on the phone. I relayed the gist of the cause of her anger to Lynn.

"The host mother claims that the student has freaked out in an upstairs bathroom and has pried the toilet off its mooring."

"Yikes," said Lynn. "That takes some doing, even for a strong and angry student."

"Yes," I replied, "and that's not all. Water from the toilet went everywhere and kept flowing because the family was out. The water supply to the house could not be shut off until they arrived home. The water has leaked through the ceiling down to the first floor, which has just been renovated. In the words of the host mother, 'Everything is ruined, and someone is going to have to pay for this'."

Lynn agreed to go over to the homestay that day, relocate the student, talk to the hosts and survey the damage. I said hopefully, "The damage can't possibly be as bad as the host mother is saying."

After his mission to the homestay, Lynn returned to the school late in the day. Little beads of sweat were showing on his forehead.

"John, you were right in saying that it's not as bad as the host mother was making out. It's worse!"

Lynn elaborated, describing that the family had a very fancy dinner table, a family heirloom that had recently been refinished. It had been seriously damaged by the water, as had the surrounding dining room and the ceiling, not to mention the bathroom and the area around it upstairs.

"It's going to take thousands of dollars to fix," Lynn projected.

"But they have insurance, surely," I responded.

"That's one of the parts of it that's worse," Lynn grimaced. "The family does not want to claim insurance as they don't want their premium to go up."

"But covering something like this is what insurance is for," I said.

"Seemingly," Lynn agreed.

Fortunately, after a lot of back and forth, Lynn was able to persuade the family to accept that they would need to claim insurance and that GV Calgary would ensure that the deductible would be covered. The student tried to walk away from any responsibility by blaming "bad plumbing". We were able to have his agent agree that the deductible amount would be taken from the partial refund we would be giving the student. We could not, in all conscience, place this student with another host and he decided to go back to his home country.

Years later, one student entered a home like a lightning strike. After the host father had picked him up at the airport, they arrived at the front door of the homestay, where the mother greeted him and politely explained, "Now in Canada, we take our shoes off at the front door. So would you mind doing that for me each time you come into the house, please?"

The student responded, "You are woman. Don't tell me what to do."

Even by the standards of a first contact gone wrong, a situation that was normally recoverable, this was debilitating. The host father called the emergency line and told our Homestay Coordinator that they could not have this student in their home.

In many cases, students and families can have a rough initial introduction and first few days together, just as students can have initial trouble settling into a school or program. Then it often becomes relatively smooth sailing. This was not the case with the student who was reluctant to take off his shoes. He was away from his country for the first time. He just could not adjust, nor did he wish to compromise. He left the school and the new homestay after just a week.

To add insult to injury, his agency had not forwarded funds. The agency principals disappeared without a trace, as we discovered when our GV Marketing Director was in their city and tried to contact them. This was a teachable moment for us in the school. We would not be so trusting about waiting for payments. We concluded that host families could not be expected to wait for their payments and that our program could not be reasonably expected to carry a debt load, with its slim margin of profit.

We learned to work with pre-arrival information and cultural training with the help of our agent partners, to orient students more effectively to their study and living experiences in Calgary. This included orientation to living in Canadian homes and demonstrating respect for host families.

In most cases, as evidenced by formal surveys and anecdotal feedback given by host families, students and agents, the GV Calgary homestay program worked well. Hosts generally related to students as if they were members of their own families. Most international students adapted and fit into households if they felt valued. Clearly, students felt more welcome as guests when their presence was at least as important to a host as the income derived from it. When hosts and others with whom students interacted took a genuine interest in students and where they were from, students usually became more comfortable about being far from home and operating in English. Stories of everyday kindnesses and people going the extra mile, such as when a city bus driver drove out of his way to find the homestay for a student in a snowstorm, were heartwarming. Communication about the many instances of hospitality enhanced Calgary's international reputation as a place to study.

Still, homestay is a constant management issue for a language business 365 days a year, 24 hours a day. There are various models for the management of a homestay program. In the early years, Global Village Calgary depended on the payments for host families to be sent from the central administration office in Vancouver. Delays caused problems, frustrations and used up a lot of time. Some chain schools have a model where the homestay programs for different locations are coordinated from another country. In my experience, homestay programs are best administered at the local level where the relevant staff build relationships with host families and students whom they can connect with in real time and counsel in person when necessary.

A revolving door of homestay coordinators can be a reality for those of us in the language business. In one three-year period, GV Calgary had three different homestay coordinators. One told me that she was quitting in less than two weeks. In exit interviews the coordinators cited many stresses, including that of finding host families for the busy season in the summer. It was especially difficult to source those who would host teens. Managing homestay is a difficult role, as program administrators must balance the needs and aspirations of host families, students, their parents and often agents. We were successful overall in hiring homestay coordinators who were highly effective, but it was a role prone to burnout.

After 18 years of operations, we looked to a new model for managing homestay at GV Calgary. Canada Homestay Network (CHN) was working with the Calgary Board of Education. I consulted with my colleague there. CHN has a model where they shared the workload among staff, founded upon core values of care for students and relationship building among all the stakeholders. The main elements, such as covering the 24/7 emergency phone and the placement process whereby students are matched with host families, as well as working directly with students and agents, were handled by a team.

It was a big call to partially outsource this service. We needed CHN to have a presence of at least one staff member in the school, to meet with students over their homestay concerns. We also wanted to retain control of the finances and work in collaboration with CHN. A key aspect was that CHN had the capacity to find host families for teenage students during the busy season. Because of the commitment and professionalism of all those involved, the hybrid model with Global Village Calgary and the Canada Homestay Network working together served the interests of the students, host families and the businesses involved.

At Global Village Calgary, we learned quickly to cover off a myriad of issues and to have clear policies for what happens under the supervision of staff. We discovered from the beginning that all involved in school programs need to ensure, as far as possible, that safety protocols and common-sense practices are followed away from campus, not only on field trips but also within homestays. It goes without saying that everyone involved is upset when something unfortunate occurs. This is often when schools are held accountable for things that we cannot control. We knew from the earliest days of GV Calgary that a culture of responsible, safety-conscious people, from school staff to host families to the service providers of activities, is essential in maintaining an overall level of heightened and necessary vigilance, especially if managers wish to get any sleep at all!

TIPS

If you are a manager:

- Engage trusted, highly competent staff, with stamina and a strong sense of care for people
- Hire homestay staff who have conflict resolution, counselling skills and profiles that fit exceedingly well with managing complexity
- Ensure that staff relate well to all stakeholders, such as students, agent partners, host families and other staff members
- Prioritize issues based on protecting the welfare of people and the interests of the business
- Ensure upfront payments for homestay
- Enlist the support of agents with pre-departure orientation of students
- Enact a model for homestay management that guards against burnout of staff and heeds organizational values, such as respect for all

Youth Programs

Throughout my experiences as a manager at a university ESL program and at Global Village, summer youth programs made me nervous because there was always a surplus of issues demanding staff time and energy. Summer was the time of the year when all the other programs were running on all cylinders as well.

Many language schools and programs depend on the revenue from youth programs and often feel the pressure to enroll students even younger than teenagers. At GV Calgary, we tried to draw the line at accepting students younger than 13 years old, because of the added burden of care and sense of responsibility placed on the school. We made exceptions, for example, for the younger siblings of students in another GV Calgary program or for the children of teen program chaperones.

We also had exceptions forced upon us, such as when an agent "made a mistake" about a Latin American girl's birthdate. She turned out to be eight rather than eleven years old as indicated on her registration form. This student wore runners with little flashing lights in their heels. These seemed to act as warning lights to draw attention to the extra vigilance needed for such a young student, as she blithely skipped around the school.

In July 2011, we had a great group of about 30 students from the central Navarro region in Spain under a three-week scholarship program. These intelligent students, all 16 and 17 years old, were impressive in their maturity and were each looking at careers like medicine and law. In reflecting on this program, I see how it demonstrated again how young people benefitted from an international student experience at an important time in their lives. The growth in their English proficiency was often exponential even in less than a month. The students also participated in sports and other activities like the Calgary Stampede and went on excursions to the Rockies. Teachers in the program, as well as staff we hired to supervise activities, noted how the teenage students from Spain and other countries engaged in the spirit of learning about different cultures and life in our Canadian city.

That year's program also displayed challenges that lurked behind the scenes. The homestay program that summer once again proved critical. Our homestay coordinator had exhausted herself placing summer students with host families and dealing with all the inevitable issues of the students, group leaders and the families.

The group was supposed to fly out on a Saturday, but it turned out that their flight was booked for the Sunday. The group leaders informed us late in their last week in Calgary about the change of plan. They thought the travel agent in Spain had made this known to us. This wasn't the case. Now homestay hosts had the students for an extra night. I had a prescient, uneasy feeling as Cathie and I left for a two-day camping trip in the Rockies.

While we hiked and enjoyed the spectacular scenery of Lake O'Hara, I could not quite relax. The instant I was within cell phone range, my Blackberry beeped like it was in cardiac arrest. I had about 40 phone calls and texts all concerning the Spanish youth program.

The Spanish group leaders were extremely concerned about a 17-year-old student who said that she had rebuffed "the overtures" of a host family father. We learned that his wife, who thought that the student would have departed Calgary by then, had arranged that evening to be out of town with friends. The student said that when the host father made a pass at her, she left and went to another homestay where a friend was staying, leaving most of her belongings behind. I had an intense, yet silent, visceral reaction to the claim that a person, whom we relied on and had vetted, would betray the trust of all concerned.

The issue of the student's belongings being picked up had been left hanging. We had no staff member available to do this. So, Cathie and I drove to the homestay and I went in to collect the student's things, after I informed them by telephone that the student would not be returning.

The host father and mother met me at the door. While the father stood at the foot of the stairs glaring at me, the mother said that she could not understand why the student had left. She said she had a gift that she wanted to give the student. I simply said that the student had left to be with her friend at another GV homestay for her last night in Calgary.

"But I want to know what's really going on," the host mother said.

"I can't comment, further," I said and added, "I'm merely here to pick up the bags, so that they can be returned to her."

The tension was unbelievably excruciating. The host father asked, "Does this mean that we will no longer be hosts for Global Village?"

Knowing full well that the answer was yes, but not wanting to add to the agony of the moment, I replied, "That's something the school will follow up with you about."

As I got back in the car, I mumbled to Cathie, "That was brutal." Nothing further needed to be said.

Later in the day, there was the inevitable conversation with the two Spanish group leaders when they came to pick up the student's luggage at our place. After all the preparation and the work in delivering the program, the agency would be made aware of the student's allegation. This proved to be the nail in the coffin for what had been a successful, multi-year program for Spanish teens at GV Calgary.

This experience highlights the complex relationship between teen programs, homestay, management, agencies, and the level of oversight required for such programs. It is often the truly unfortunate and rare events that stick out amid the positive. For the organization, I found it important to keep things in perspective. However, I shiver with regret every time I think of students who had negative experiences.

Some who manage and market language businesses may argue that any income, no matter how slender, is worth the effort. Program leaders need to ask themselves and their marketing people questions about the efficacy and risk versus the rewards of those margins.

In contrast to the few sad incidents, many uplifting stories have been related to me over the years when host families in Calgary and Victoria have hosted members of the same family at different times and even enjoyed reciprocal visits to the families of students in countries all over the world. As a shining example, Paula at GV Victoria informed me that a Guatemalan teen group in 2007 wanted to include a boy, Hector, who was only 11 years old, and too young be in the care of any GV Victoria host family. Paula and her family very generously volunteered to host. The next year, Paula, her partner, and their son travelled to Guatemala City to visit the student and his family. Then, in 2015, Hector's sister, Annelise, stayed with Paula's family while studying at GV Victoria. Surely, the family and cultural bonds formed through such rich international exchange experiences over many years stand as a gold-standard measure for our programs.

TIPS

If you are a manager:

- Analyse the risks and the costs before embarking on youth programs
- Allow for staff resources, time and expertise to deliver quality homestay experiences
- Remember that duty of care is paramount
- Prepare for crisis scenarios in your team's planning
- Prepare to improvise to solve problems when unexpected events occur

Easier Said Than Done

Relocating the school

I was filled with dread as 2002 progressed. Global Village Calgary's lease in Gulf Canada Square would end on December 31, 2002 and we were going to have to move. I tried not to feel overwhelmed by the scope of the project that I would have to coordinate.

GV Calgary was going well. We had established a solid international student base with supportive agents who were enrolling students from across the globe. Each year we ran the roller coaster of low enrollment (approximately 125 students over the Christmas and New Year to our summer capacity of 225). Several times, we had to lease extra space for July, the busiest month of the year.

It was the end of April when I turned my attention to finding new digs for the school. Fortunately, five years earlier, I had met an excellent commercial real estate broker, Don Rempel. We scoured the city for likely premises and finally settled on one of the heritage buildings in downtown Calgary.

It was a four-story building, built in 1911, called the North West Travellers' (NWT) Building. It stood in the eastern part of the downtown core, opposite a park that was home to memorable public art named the "Learning Statues". It was only two blocks from a light rail train station. The building had lots of exterior windows that were perfect for classrooms. As a bonus, from the outside, it had the stately look of a college.

The NWT Building was to have three different owners during our tenure there. When we signed the original lease, the developer-owner was fixing up the building's exterior with new windows, painting and masonry work in accordance with provincial heritage standards. The problem was that it was derelict on the inside. The building had previously been used as a Salvation Army hostel but had stood vacant for over three years. The interior would have to be completely gutted and redesigned. There was over 16,700 square feet (1,550 square metres) of space, giving us more room than our Gulf Canada Square location and the opportunity to design a modern language school in a local heritage site.

We planned to have capacity for 300 students. On three floors we had space for up to 25 classrooms, including two computer labs and an expanded student lounge area. The expansion in capacity and facilities was a business risk, but calculated and manageable, as I explained to the other board members. Our student enrollment had been increasing as Canada became a more popular language destination. We were partly benefitting from the uncertainty in the US market following the 9/11 attacks.

Don, our broker, presciently noted that the large parking lot to the immediate west of the NWT Building would likely be used for a high-rise office development within the next five years. Despite my worries about future construction interrupting our business, the lease in the NWT Building was our best option. GV Calgary signed a ten-year lease with a further five-year option.

True to prediction, our neighbour's construction began in 2007 and in 2010 The Bow was completed. At 58 stories high, it soared 236 metres above us. Because of its interesting architecture and public art, the location became a tourist attraction. Although I was concerned about the potential for noise, the west sheer brick wall of the NWT Building and the gap between us and The Bow buffered the sounds and vibrations of the construction.

Overseeing our renovation in the new space and preparing to relocate Global Village Calgary was a huge project. The landlord had granted a leasehold improvement allowance as part of the deal, essentially handing us the shell of the space with permission to develop it.

By the time we had the plans approved and the managing contractor selected, we had just over three months for the trades to build out the space. We were due to vacate our location in Gulf Canada Square by December 31, 2002. Not only were the deadlines tight, but it also turned out that I had to manage the Construction Manager, too.

In addition to working on the plans, I had to gain the permission of GV's Managing Director in Vancouver on issues like the size of classrooms and where the teachers' room would be located. Altogether, this made for a set of engaging but taxing tasks. I insisted that the teachers have an ample room on the 4th floor with outside windows. The space for the teachers was well integrated in the overall design, with my hope that a pleasant workspace would keep people happier.

The issue of how many washrooms to include in the new space was part of the negotiations with the landlord. Washroom facilities in language schools are often a contentious issue. In Gulf Canada Square, we had only one set of washrooms. Students and staff complained regularly about their inadequacy. I tried to tune out the aggravated cries about what was going on in the washrooms and joined the few on the administrative staff who added the use of toilet plungers to our job descriptions.

I was determined to have men and women's washrooms on each of the three floors of our new space. When the landlord baulked at this, I dug in. "Is this a deal breaker?" he asked.

"Yes," I responded. "We can have the best-looking space of any language school going, but the school with the most washrooms is the most practical."

The landlord conceded this important point and we moved ahead.

Through the second half of 2002, my life was consumed with the planning and building project. Meanwhile, our Gulf Canada Square landlord made it clear that they did not want GV Calgary as tenants. If the new school premises were not ready, we certainly were not going to be able to run classes in a public park in the middle of winter.

A month out, it was clear that the new space would not be ready by January 1, 2003. However, there was a clause in the lease stating that the landlord had to provide financial relief if the space was not ready for occupancy on time. So, I explained the situation about the new space not being ready to the representative for the landlord in Gulf Canada Square. I made the case that Gulf Canada Square would make some more revenue from our occupancy of a further two weeks, and noted the fact that they did not have another tenant ready to move in. We settled on $10,000 which the landlord of our new space agreed to pay. We had a stay of a vital, extra two weeks. Despite the unpopularity of Global Village Calgary with most other tenants, we were grateful for the extension. Even then, I was feeling nervous about the deadlines.

An interior designer had drawn up plans for the new space, based on my input. The design of the new space was good, but we ended up with some odd-shaped rooms. This was because late in the process the Fire Chief insisted on a ringed stairwell around the elevator shaft. The original elevator was also being replaced by the landlord.

Fortunately, GV Calgary's Director of Studies and the Head Teacher both kept things running smoothly within the school, while I trotted between Gulf Canada Square and the North West Travellers' Building.

It was a brisk, but therapeutic, 15-minute walk. Often, Terry O'Dwyer would accompany me. Terry, the big garrulous Newfoundlander, full of jokes and repartee, had joined GV Calgary as a teacher in July 1996. Several years later he left the school and briefly worked as a foreman in a Calgary factory. This was not a good fit for him and he asked to return to GV Calgary. I received him back with open arms.

Terry was now teaching and providing IT support, which we had found necessary to manage at the local level. Despite his obvious misgivings that the space would not be ready, Terry literally walked alongside me on the project, by coordinating some of the IT set-up, which was still being orchestrated in theory from GV Vancouver. Terry summed up the situation. We agreed that he needed to be the man on the ground in Calgary to deal with the electrical and cabling issues for our IT. My circuits would have burned out if I had taken that on.

By Christmas Eve, we were down to the wire. The place did not look like it would be ready by mid-January. We would get no further consideration from Gulf Canada Square. While checking on the new space, I spoke to one of the trade guys on the afternoon of December 24. He said, "Well, I'm off for Christmas and New Year. See you in two weeks."

My heart skipped a few beats. There was absolutely no way the space would be ready if the trades were taking a full two weeks off now. I called the Construction Manager, who sounded like he was fully immersed in liquid Christmas cheer. His initial resistance gave way, after I explained the reality of the situation. He assured me that work would be done on the business days during the holiday period.

I took another brisk walk back to Gulf Canada Square. Cathie picked me up outside the building with the boys and Christmas presents loaded in the car. We took off for her parents' farm, where I tried to relax. I felt exhausted. But I recognized that it was time to be present for my family and to enjoy Christmas without dwelling on what the first few weeks of 2003 would be like.

With or without my obsessing, the first two weeks of 2003 turned out to be frenetic. Most staff rallied to support Global Village Calgary's transition to our new home. I tried to keep my head above water, even though I felt I was swimming against an overwhelming, incoming tide. The new space was not going to be completely prepared for occupancy by the time we moved the school in mid-January. Inevitably, there would be trades people still completing key tasks. Nevertheless, we had placated the concerns of the Fire Chief and other City of Calgary officials. We had permission to move in, even though there were many details that needed to be covered off.

We ploughed ahead with our plans. The walks between Gulf Canada Square and the North West Travellers' Building became more urgent as Terry and I checked on the state of the work. On one gut-wrenching day, about ten days out from the move, on the first business day after New Year's, the Construction Manager informed me that the communications company would not have our phone and data connected for a further six weeks. Apparently, the work order, including the installation for updated cabling to the heritage building, had sat on a supervisor's desk for weeks and not been passed along.

We had been marketing the relocation of Global Village Calgary as a relocation into a state-of the-art modern language facility with web-enabled classrooms. As we walked quickly along Stephen Avenue after I received this news, I told Terry I felt like doing a full dying cockroach routine by lying down on my back and clawing at the air in frustration. More practically, I had to get to work as I was not going to let this stand. There was just no way we could operate without phones and computers for such an extended period.

By marshalling the voices of the Landlord and the Construction Manager in support, we received reluctant agreement to get the line work done in time. After another round of permissions from the City of Calgary, a section of road and frozen earth underneath 5th Avenue, next to the new school, was dug up on a wintery Saturday. The new cable lines were installed. We would have phones and data.

We arranged for the teachers to make a quick tour of the new space in the week prior to the move, so that they could see the new digs. We also encouraged staff to talk up the advantages of the new location when they directed students there for the first day. We were going to finish classes on Friday morning in Gulf Canada Square, move everything over the weekend and set up to start classes in the new building on Monday. It was going to be extremely tight.

We had contracted a small moving company. Their crew of four people plus five of us from the school were there to do the heavy lifting. Fortunately, the weather was not as cold as it could be in Calgary at that time of year.

Unexpected snags kept appearing though. We had the first one on Friday night when a head janitor locked off the freight elevator in Gulf Canada Square. To lose time like this was infuriating and with my blood pressure rising, I gave the person responsible a verbal blast. My uncharacteristic moment was witnessed by the moving company guys. They could see I was wired tight and proceeded to perform their tasks with alacrity over the weekend.

I was incredibly lucky that key members of staff stepped up. Terry was a tower of strength. The Director of Studies and the Head Teacher helped immensely by making sure the teachers only had two boxes each to move over. I asked the Head Teacher to devise a seating plan so that teachers would be given a designated spot in the teachers' room. It was all hands-on deck.

We had to pare things back in the old space and be selective in what we relocated. Old furniture that did not make the cut for the new space and that was too old to be sold had to be carted to the garbage dump. After midnight on Friday, when the loading dock to Gulf Canada Square was closed despite our understanding it would be left open, I had no recourse but to park a large rental van in front of the building. At 1:00 am, a zealous policeman left me a parking ticket for $150.

We worked over the weekend with the moving men, along with a small cadre of school staff and spouses. Some of us had put in shifts of 12 to 16 hours for five days and nights straight. I remember the lights of the almost silent downtown Calgary in the wee hours of consecutive winter mornings. I made repeated drives to Spyhill Landfill on the outskirts of Calgary, where there were seagulls chortling in an eerie fog as I discarded things from the school. Such sights and sounds contributed to the surreal nature of the weekend.

Monday, opening day, arrived. It had been a weekend of little sleep. The tiles were still being laid by contractors on the stairwell as we opened in the morning. People had to step gingerly around them or use the elevator. Exhausted but victorious, we welcomed new and continuing students, about 200 in all.

I had not been confident that all was well with the elevator installation because for weeks the landlord had been having serious, hushed conversations with contractors every time I came into the building. Sure enough, on the first morning, the elevator froze between floors. Ten students and two teachers were stuck for about 30 minutes before they were rescued. This cranked up the stress. As it turned out, the elevator was immobilized four times during our first year in the new space. Each time the elevator stuck, anxiety levels soared.

On the first day, we were busy dodging other bullets. Some of the students said they preferred the old space as they thought that the building, to which we had moved, was too old. The heritage character of the building, not to mention the complete renovation we had undertaken, seemed lost on them. I started to feel like I was in a Monty Python episode and could feel my inner John Cleese rising to the surface. I was almost prepared to break out a silly walk and say, "Well, let's just pack everything up and move back to the old building then." Instead, I kept my distance from the negative students.

Years before, I had learned the hard lesson during already tough days not to invite confrontation with students. Once, in Gulf Canada Square, I had challenged a Latin American student about not making any effort to speak English in the student lounge. By calling him out in front of his friends and using the wrong tone, I lit a match. The incident blew up in my face with the student yelling back at me. In fact, I learned to avoid confronting students at all, if possible, and especially not in front of their fellow students. I resolved that in the new space, I would be calmer and strive for positivity in any interaction, even when students were being difficult.

Even on a bad day, I found I could trip myself back into having a better day by not over-reacting. On that first day in the new space, riddled with aching muscles and fatigue from lack of sleep, I needed to make a special effort to stay calm, as difficulties kept arising and negative comments were flying around.

Change was in the air, both metaphorically speaking and in reality. Throughout the first day in the new space, there was a slight toxic smell emanating from the new carpet squares that had just been glued down over the weekend. One of the host mothers had accompanied her student to the first day at school and she kept popping up throughout the day. "What's that smell?" she asked in the morning. Then she repeated the same question more stridently when she came by in the lunch hour to check on the student and finally again when she came by at the end of the day to pick her up. I appreciated the diligence of the host mother in looking after her student. However, having this repeated throughout the day became a negative mantra playing in my head. As she was leaving with the student and passing the reception area near my office, she offered one parting shot, "I'd really like to know what that smell is."

She had been told it was the carpet glue and that we had been assured that its odour would dissipate in a few days. Fortunately, this turned out to be the case. Yet the echo of this irritating comment added to all the upheaval of the day. I'm afraid I cracked. While trying to maintain a smile, which I am sure came across more like a grimace, I introduced myself to the homestay mother. I thanked her for her work with students and said, "By the way, that smell you keep asking about, is the smell of success."

Eventually, the tumultuous first day was done. As I slumped home, I thought of the joke about what the child said to his mother after his first day at school. Over supper with Cathie and the boys, I said,

"Well, I made it through. But I'm still going to have to go back tomorrow!"

Sometimes the thoughts anticipating what might happen are not as bad as the reality. Even when things do not go well, there seems to be a momentum to getting through things if you take a deep breath, keep your head, and just plough on. Sometimes, you simply must struggle harder.

On the wider Global Village front, changes were also in the air. Yet, at Global Village Calgary, we had managed the move, enrollment was good, and we started receiving lots of positive comments about the new space. There was the inevitable negativity from some quarters, like agents overseas saying that they had heard from their student clients that the school was still under construction. I tried to focus on the big picture while taking care of the details and not getting too bogged down in them. The positive energy of most staff members and students was a huge plus.

By March 2003, drained by the ordeal of relocating the school and by the long winter, it was time to head out of Calgary to Australia for some warmth. As the plane took off, it banked over the downtown core, as if bidding adieu. I had a perfect view from the air of the top of the North West Travellers' Building. How peaceful and cozy the school looked under a thin layer of snow covering its roof, like a child tucked into bed under a warm, white blanket. I thought of the maelstrom of activity that it had taken to build out and move into the space, and the daily interactions that were happening in every classroom even as I flew over. It was reassuring to think that it was all worthwhile.

TIPS

If you are a teacher or an administrative staff member:

- Remember that all staff are under pressure during periods of change and be supportive

- Don't get distracted by minor details

- Focus on key goals and the value of your work with students

If you are a manager:

- Remember that all staff are under pressure during periods of change and some will respond more positively than others

- Seek professional expertise in areas like new leases and avoid the false economy of saving money by trying to be an expert on such matters

- Read the fine print of contracts very carefully and revisit during a project

- Ensure you have prepared a project management team to work with you and have a communication strategy with the whole staff about a project like relocating premises

- Plough on and strive for positivity and practical solutions in interactions, no matter how fraught

- Pick your battles

Team Vibrations

When I was a manager at the University of Lethbridge and later at Global Village Calgary, I was determined to create a positive and professional environment for all. I wished to attract and retain appropriately-trained staff members who genuinely wanted to help people. I also reasoned that if my colleagues saw the setting as a pleasant place in which to work and explore their career goals, then we could all carry on more cheerfully and effectively. Following the same logic, I thought that students would also be attracted to the school and feel part of a cohesive learning community.

At its heart, a language business is people-based. During the hubbub of daily work, we are constantly reminded that the social contexts for how people relate and the work settings themselves are fluid. As with many businesses, a language business must be responsive and adaptive to local, national and international environments.

Associations like Languages Canada (LC) and the International Association of Language Centres (IALC) set the standards for their language program members and conduct regular evaluations. These standards include requirements for hiring teachers and administration staff, professional development plans, curriculum guidelines, homestay and other accommodation-related policies, provisions for youth students, facilities standards, as well safety and activities in the community. Certainly, all the policies are important. But in looking beyond the nuts and bolts, I believe that good vibrations are emblematic of a highly functional learning community. Thus, we sought opportunities to build a positive atmosphere not only with the daily interactions inside the school, but with other events too.

At GV Calgary we were fortunate to have the annual Calgary Stampede in early July, the peak of the summer business. Not only did we promote it through our marketing, we also used it as a staff team-building exercise and general raising of spirits. Many students and teachers dressed as cowboys and cowgirls for the whole ten-day event. We made memories and most had fun.

The Stampede Parade which was held on the first Friday of July tested the mettle of our staff each year. We relied on experienced teachers to orient new teachers and the students, before allowing our classes to leave the safe confines of the school and mingle with the thousands of parade viewers from Calgary and around the globe. Our receptionist became operation central, with knowledge of where the classes were staked out along the parade route in case students got lost in the crowds and needed to be redirected. The pay-off was that students, accompanied by their teachers and classmates, spoke with locals and visitors alike, pressed through the crowded sidewalks, saw laidback Canadian crowd control in action, and usually got into the spirit of the day. Getting everyone safely back to class in a timely fashion was one of the challenges, and well worth the effort.

Right from the initial interview, I believe it is possible for managers of a language business to set the expectations for everyone to step up and contribute to the soul of the workplace. We learned to set the tone when interviewing new staff by letting potential hires know that they were expected to be cooperative colleagues. Determining whether a potential staff member is a good "fit" with the team is a central consideration when interviewing and vetting job candidates. I also liked to explore the congruence between an individual's expectations for career growth and the realities of the overall program.

It seems obvious that potential hires should conduct some research into the organization. In interviews, I often wondered aloud what the interviewee knew about Global Village. On rare occasions, the response was, "Nothing really."

"You haven't even looked at our web site?" was my thought bubble. "Well then, let's go for a tour."

The school tour allowed the potential recruit to observe the school in operation, but also to make comments and ask questions. For me, this situation was a window into motivation and character. I also found that having other staff members show potential hires around the school offered bonus insights during impromptu moments. A Head Teacher once reported to me that on such a tour, a male applicant showed undue interest in the female students, with a comment about the good-looking women in classes. This was a red flag. Even though he did well in his formal interview and his resume ticked all the boxes, there would be no job offer for him.

We were also looking for staff who could manage conflict effectively. I found it illuminating to ask people how they had handled a conflict in a work setting. Interestingly, they often chose to share how they handled a tricky issue if they had worked overseas. That was relevant. In my view, this question was better than a hypothetical one, as people could reference a real experience, consider how they dealt with it, and be authentic.

Naturally, there is a strong obligation to be careful about whom we hire. Police record checks on staff and host families are now common best practices. I learned to always do the reference checks. Looking into gaps in a potential hire's resume can be telling, for example, if she or he has not listed the last employer as a reference.

I also found responses enlightening when I asked a final open-ended question to the person offering the reference, "Is there anything else you can tell me about this person?" I remember Lynn reporting that he asked that question when he was doing a reference check. The Director of Studies at the other school replied, "Well there was that incident with that teacher kissing a student at a bar, but I don't want to talk about that." That was a telling response.

Where underage students are being schooled, more explicit questions are mandatory. For example, there are legal ramifications if one excludes certain questions in a reference check such as, "To your knowledge, is there anything in the applicant's actions or behaviour that would make them unsuitable for working with children?"

Yet interviews and reference checks alone do not provide the nuanced understanding of whether a new hire will add value to a school. Our gold-standard approach to adding a new teacher included an interview, reference checks, a school tour, an initial informal introduction to other staff members, and an observed practice lesson. At GV Calgary, we were fortunate to also have evidence of new teachers' expertise, based on recommendations from our CELTA tutors.

Ongoing observations and feedback from senior staff and student feedback have their place, too, when it comes to teachers improving their craft. Regular evaluations by students and staff colleagues commenced soon after teachers joined GV and continued regularly (and at least annually for all staff members). We also found it productive to encourage self-reflection by staff about how their work was going.

At Global Village locations, students and staff had opportunities to evaluate aspects of the school as well. This was not only with respect to the broad program areas of academics, accommodation and activities but we noted formal survey responses and more informal feedback about elements like perceptions of friendliness and professionalism in services to students. When we invited teachers and administrative staff at GV Calgary and GV Victoria to have direct input into updates of our policy manuals, it was a good opportunity to gather feedback on how the school was being administered. We all needed to be open to constructive conversations.

We also learned that it was important to have leaders at all levels of the organisation. I greatly valued the unassuming, quiet achievers in the teachers' room. Greg for example, was about 50 years old when he completed CELTA training at GV Calgary and then joined our staff. Greg is a writer and, as with many people who come to teach English, has an eclectic resume. He has also lived from coast to coast in Canada, from Halifax to Victoria. Greg's mature outlook, breadth of experiences and obvious care for the students, found a natural home in the classroom. He was also a calming staff room presence and looked out for his colleagues. Teachers such as Greg were instrumental in making the teachers' room a sanctuary rather than a breeding ground for discontent.

We found that it helped if there was a balanced mix of workers, combining veterans who offer mentorship and stability with younger employees who bring fresh ideas and energy. No matter where people are in their overall career trajectories or in their specific roles within the school, we felt strongly that the whole enterprise benefitted when staff members were willing to continue to learn and to support one another.

Other teachers, including those who are newly established, could also assist others compassionately and practically. They may have had their own initial difficulties becoming oriented and into the flow and demands of teaching at GV Calgary. Just a few minutes sharing a lesson idea could be abundantly beneficial and encouraging for a new teacher.

I reflected a lot on what happens when the inevitable problems appear in relationships involving staff. The line of least resistance is to take a hands-off approach and let people work it out for themselves. In doing so, we hope they resolve naturally, but sometimes they do not. If people were disturbing their colleagues or relating to students in a way that undercut the positive atmosphere, I had to weigh up where my intervention or that of another supervisor might be needed. I learned the hard way that things can fester if they're not attended to. I also learned that actions in such circumstances must be strategic, fair and timely.

At both University of Lethbridge and GV Calgary, there were times that I would beat myself up and spend sleepless hours in contemplation of the ways staff members could upset one another. Often the staff members themselves were oblivious to the disruption that they were causing. In such cases, I approached them quietly and diplomatically, in attempts to make sure that things did not degrade.

I arrived at what I believed is an important question early in my managerial career: what messages are managers sending if they allow dysfunction, caused by just a small minority, to continue? While I believe in building bridges wherever possible, there are times when unhappy persons prompt their own exit by burning bridges. There can be clarity for all in the bright light of such conflagrations. On one memorable occasion, after we informed a teacher that we could not renew her contract, she demonstrated why this was the right decision when she vented her hostility and spewed invective at her colleagues, including me, while she stormed out of the school.

Like most people, I am not a fan of confrontation. All of us have things going on in our personal lives that we need to compartmentalize and separate from our work lives. I was attuned to the reality that good people who turned into troublesome or poor performing employees were often facing difficulties in their private lives, and possibly even experiencing mental and physical wellness issues. I sought ways to support such staff members, sometimes in the form of offering leave or helping them realign their workdays and duties, without the organization having to terminate their employment.

Thankfully, it was only in rare instances that I found it necessary for the good of building or consolidating a team, to say goodbye to someone who had become a divisive influence. On several occasions, senior teachers or administrative staff members came forward quietly after the fact and claimed that things were actually worse than what managers were aware of. We learned that it was less likely that we would be left in the dark when all staff valued the positive culture of the school and did not want to see it deteriorate.

Tensions can simmer beneath the surface and mitigate against team building within any organization. Within each language school or program where I worked, I observed what I think of as "the creative tension" between those on the teaching side and those on the administrative side. In my opinion, administrative staff ought to consider the challenges faced by teachers while instructors should also consider the scope of responsibilities of administrative staff. Many stresses for and with students percolate below the surface with staff in discrete areas like homestay and the classroom and are not always visible to colleagues. I found that crossover staff meetings, that created time and space for both teachers and administrative staff to communicate about general problems in their program areas, could be beneficial if privacy was also safeguarded.

As a result of such staff meetings, we were able to improve communication across the school and discuss scenarios when staff members should flag issues and refer them to colleagues. For example, a teacher might be told a biased story by a student about a homestay experience. We built collective recognition that in that situation, it was best for the teacher to encourage the student to see homestay staff, to whom the teacher should also give a heads up. The homestay department invariably would have a greater grasp of the overall context as well as the ability to deal with issues.

Cross training can also prove beneficial. One way this might be achieved is by having experienced teachers assigned some administration as complementary to their instructional roles in areas such as curriculum planning and advising students on pathways.

In the narrow-margin businesses of language programs, most managers find that we can often only budget for one person in each administrative position. Often those roles will be blended with other responsibilities. When Cathie had worked at the Technical

Resource Centre in Calgary in the late 1980s, her insightful supervisor had told her that a manager should always have people cross-trained so that you have back up or "built-in redundancy" in an organization. Both Cathie and I took that concept on board. I was always on the lookout for staff members, especially among the teaching staff, who could fill admin roles.

I came to understand from my earliest years as a manager that cross-training also served to insulate the day-to-day running of the program against the inevitable upheaval of staff changes. In 2006 this lesson was reaffirmed when our Director of Studies, who was also the IELTS manager, made a career move after seven years with us. The next year our registrar, an 11-year veteran, with whom I had worked since Lethbridge days, followed her to Bow Valley College. Personally, I was happy for them with their career changes, yet I had learned to prepare for when people leave.

I looked for new people with administrative acumen, but in Global Village we usually searched among our existing staff for those who could take on administrative roles. Those already on GV Calgary staff came with in-built knowledge and experience of the fast-paced nature of our specific business and the demands of our students, agents and other stakeholders. At the same time, I needed to be aware of the signs of overtaxing responsibilities and burnout in staff. I learned to include myself in this reflection.

A specific example of the value I associated with cross-training and finding the right people to fit various roles in a language program comes from that time in 2006 when our Director of Studies left. Tania, who had joined GV Calgary in February 2000, was highly effective as a Business English teacher. A very charismatic and positive person, Tania also has an instinctive recognition of the business side of the school, especially appreciating the importance of good customer services for students. In September 2006, Tania moved into the Director of Programs position. Jackie, who had been teaching with us for five years, became our very capable IELTS Centre Manager. Jacqueline, who had been teaching at

GV Calgary since before we moved from Gulf Canada Square, assumed Head Teacher duties in support of both Tania and Jackie. Circumstances and cross-training gave GV Calgary a progressive trio of senior managers with their hearts in both teaching and approaches to administrative services. The approach worked well for us.

We took other initiatives to team build over the long haul at GV Calgary. The annual staff Christmas Party might seem an obvious way to support staff and boost morale. But that was not always the case. On one occasion, alcohol and a disagreement over a social issue fueled a heated argument between a staff member and an instructor's partner. Another time, there was a teacher who vociferously complained that we didn't pay for her partner's meal, like they did at his oil company's event. I had a quiet conversation with the teacher to explain the business context for the financing of the Christmas meal. Still, she failed to hide her resentment from other colleagues or me. The spirit of goodwill was contaminated that season as a result.

During the ebbs and flow of the seasons, and throughout my career, I have felt a strong duty to recognize the challenges staff face. I believe it is the duty of managers to be empathetic and to lay out expectations while eliciting staff buy in to achieve organizational goals. I also feel that managers, who are in positions of influence and who are mandated to make profit in private enterprise or generate funds in public institutions, should balance those pressures with advocating for living wages for staff members and for other initiatives that advance the careers of staff. I have found that people and organizations can renew their sense of purpose as a team and find resilience in hard times when they have a sense that they and their workplace are not stagnating. For retention of quality staff, good vibrations are not enough. Appropriate remuneration and professional development opportunities are necessary.

TIPS

If you are a teacher or an administrative staff member:

- Research the institution or school where you are applying for work
- Demonstrate a positive desire to help the organization as well as to develop your career
- Expect a settling-in period and welcome constructive advice
- Give back and assist new employees
- Stay attuned to the roles of others

If you are a manager:

- Set potential hires at ease and lead meaningful conversations about their experiences and career aspirations as well as goals of the program
- Ask interviewees about times in their careers when they navigated conflict with co-workers
- Encourage potential hires to take brief tours of the setting and elicit feedback from staff who accompany them
- Do your homework on reference and police checks
- Elicit opportunities for teachers and admin staff to increase their awareness of the distinct nature of each other's work
- Create opportunities for staff to cross-train and fit with other roles
- Expect cycles when employee enthusiasm, including your own, may wane and be open to ideas about building morale

Marketing Ups and Downs

The international language business is highly competitive and to survive, a language school or program obviously requires a critical mass of students. One way to achieve this is to be part of a group of schools that can share marketing costs. The addition of new school locations to organizations large or small is usually aimed at building brand identity, increasing enrollment and strengthening all the businesses in the group.

This was the case with Global Village English Centres, with its five core schools (four in Canada and one in Hawaii) that generally maintained thriving businesses from 2000 to 2020. However, a shift in branding, with the Shane Global Village (SGV) alliance in 2003 to 2004, was a negative disruptor for the GV schools. It exposed the unintended negative consequences of re-branding with a myriad of administrative headaches for managers and marketers, as well as confusion in the marketplace with our agent partners.

As the SGV alliance exemplified, attempts to expand the GV brand in fact diluted it when it was mixed with another. Further, the marketing for the group of SGV schools (five GV schools and five Shane English schools) did not meet the goal of bringing in more students for each school.

Here's a bit of corporate history. Global Village English Centres (GVEC) Inc. was formed as a marketing company in 1994. Within GV, we usually referred to it as Global Village (or GV) Marketing. The two founding schools were The Language Workshop (doing business as Global Village Toronto) which joined forces with West Coast English Language Centre (WELC doing business as GV Vancouver). The Language Workshop started in 1979 while WELC commenced operations in 1989.

Global Village Marketing was formed as a non-profit entity to help these separate school enterprises find economies of scale in marketing. Synergies were planned and evolved whereby the Toronto and Vancouver schools shared and leveraged relationships with agents across the globe. "Global Village" resonated as a brand representing an overall mission of bringing students together from diverse nationalities to study English.

The Global Village concept included the addition of new schools, of which GV Calgary was the first. The group's goals targeted profitability at each school through shared marketing costs, to create a high-quality brand that was recognized by students and agents around the world.

GV Calgary and GV Victoria were Global Village schools from their inception. They commenced operations in 1996 and 2000 respectively. Alternatively, a pre-existing school could join the group as was the case with the GV school in Hawaii in 1997. Each GV school was separately incorporated with different owners. There was crossover, with some of the principals having an interest in several schools as the group expanded. For example, I negotiated minority shares that Cathie and I purchased in the Global Village schools in Calgary and Victoria.

Global Village schools shared a similar philosophy of promoting and constantly striving for excellence in the areas of language teaching and related services. Each school needed to survive as a business on its own merits. In the early years of GV Calgary, our services included instruction in English, homestay and activities for students, and in 2003 added Cambridge CELTA (Certificate in English Language Teaching to Adults) teacher training.

In June 2005, GV Calgary started IELTS[9] testing as another revenue stream, after we signed a test centre contract with IDP[10]/ IELTS Australia, one of the international partners who delivered

---
9   International English language testing system (IELTS)
10 International Development Program (IDP)

IELTS. It had taken 18 months from the time I initiated the application to become an IELTS test centre. We satisfied the concerns of IDP/IELTS Australia about running tests according to rigorous protocols. We found common ground by aligning with the Australian organization which was keen to increase its testing capacity in Canada.

Before GV became an IELTS centre in Calgary, there was only one IELTS centre west of Winnipeg and that was in Vancouver. GV Calgary was in fact the first private sector school in Canada to be an official IELTS centre. Over the next few years, GV schools in Toronto, Vancouver and Victoria added IELTS centres to their portfolios. This meant that IELTS testing could be marketed as an innovative program for GV schools in Canada.

I sought out IELTS testing as part of the overall strategy to increase business. This was a classic "blue ocean strategy"[11], where a business adds a new component to its operations when competitors are not in that segment of the market. Of course, in keeping with the metaphor, the unpopulated and comparative quietude of the blue part of the ocean will likely be inhabited by others and turn red sooner or later. If there is opportunity, others will sniff it out like sharks because fierce competition is the name of the game.

Around the period when GV Calgary relocated in January 2003 and I was looking at ways to boost programs and enrollment, the winds of change had also been blowing across Global Village for over a year. I first heard of a change in our identity in 2001 when GV Vancouver's School Manager called me and asked me what I knew about the Shane group joining Global Village. He directed my attention to the GV website where an announcement had just popped up saying that Global Village was pleased to announce a strategic alliance with the Shane English Schools. "Shane Global Village English Centres" would include the current GV locations plus the Shane English schools in the UK (London, Oxford and

---

[11] W. Chan Kim and Renée Mauborgne, *Blue Ocean Strategy* (2004)

a new one to open in Hastings) as well as in Auckland, New Zealand and Cape Town, South Africa.

We quickly figured out that GV's Managing Director had not consulted the individual schools through their boards or managers. He had made the decision with the assent of most of the shareholders and the directors of GV Marketing.

In April 2002, I went to Brazil for the first time. The representatives from the Global Village schools as well as those from the Shane English schools convened for a week in a hotel that was in a compound outside the city of Campinas in Sao Paulo state. The meetings were about the marketing of the combined Shane Global Village schools for the inaugural year of the alliance.

The managers from all the GV and Shane schools, as well as marketing staff from the two groups, all got on famously. We shared similar outlooks and values in terms of how we saw our schools running and being represented. At the end of intense meetings each day, we shared laughs over drinks and rambunctious volleyball games in the hotel pool. During the second week, we paid visits to agents in cities such as Sao Paulo and Belo Horizonte.

Mikio, a new partner from Sydney, Australia, joined the group and we met for the first time. Like many in the language industry, Mikio had a compelling personal story, having gone from his native Japan to study English in Tasmania in the 1970s. Along with his wife, Mikio had opened a school in Sydney in 1988. Mikio joined the group to expand his student base, not only for Sydney, but also for the new school he was looking to open in Brisbane. He was looking for others to go in on the project. I harboured thoughts that I might one day work again in Australia or have business interests there. With his Brisbane initiative, Mikio gave me the opportunity to explore the latter.

Within the combination of the Global Village network and the Shane English Schools, the managers of the schools and the marketing staff mostly saw eye to eye. Yet, there were those who quietly expressed the opinion that the Shane Global Village concept was not going to work for long. One reason was that the two men at the top were cut from a different cloth, and it did not seem that they shared the same vision of how the marketing and administration of the group of schools would mesh. While we hoped that Shane English schools would benefit from GV's market presence in Asia and Latin America and that GV schools would benefit from Shane's agents in Europe, the practicalities behind the theory were not fully researched.

The agreement with Shane English Schools went ahead based on a memorandum of understanding which would be revisited after it was signed for an initial year, effective January 2003. I loved the name Global Village as it encapsulated the spirit of bringing international students together in our schools. I thought adding "Shane" at the front would dilute the brand and cause confusion. I was not alone with that thought as other school managers and board directors also expressed reservations. All our signage and materials would have to be redone. That alone was not a trivial task. While the practicalities of school administration within GV Calgary remained much the same, a lot of energy was expended explaining the change in name to staff, students and strategic stakeholders like our agent partners.

By May 2003, serious questions were being asked about the future of the Shane Global Village alliance at the meeting of school representatives and marketing staff in Vancouver. In addition, the Managing Director (MD) announced that he was resigning from that role with GV Vancouver and GV Marketing. Soon, he would also step down as MD of SGV, GV Calgary and GV Victoria.

The meetings in May 2003 proceeded for several days with discussions about the marketing of the group and planning for 2004. The economies of scale and the increasing enrollment of students that GV Schools had gained in the period before the Shane alliance, were not being duplicated for the GV or for all the Shane English schools. It was proving to be administratively unwieldy as well as expensive to market a group of ten schools in different English-speaking countries. Agents sometimes wondered aloud why Global Village had aligned with Shane English Schools, who were better known to them as a group with many small schools across Japan. However, Shane's schools in Japan and elsewhere in Asia were outside the SGV alliance.

In fact, the five Global Village schools lost ground with the SGV branding. While in essence nothing really changed in the day-to-day of the school cycle of programs, curriculum and classroom methods, the GV marketers had to reassure and explain the alliance and brand change to the agents. The marketers' attention and message for each school location was also diluted because they were now pitching ten schools instead of five. Focus became diffused in the overall marketing effort, and the original goal of bringing more students into each school was not being met.

After the 2003 meetings in Vancouver, I made my way to the airport on a shining spring morning. An air of desolation hung over the city though, as the Vancouver Canucks NHL[12] team had lost Game 7 the night before. There is something quintessentially Canadian in losing the decisive Game 7 in the hockey playoffs. Losses are bitterly felt but Canadians are pragmatic in their hopes for better fortune for their teams "next year". I also felt that better times were ahead for Global Village schools.

The week after the Vancouver meetings, I received an email from the MD in which he noted that he was resigning from GV Calgary. He was also resigning as a director on the board. He wished me well.

This meant that I was to be GV Calgary's President and CEO[13] and board chair. Any doubts I had about remaining with GV had been cleared away and I looked to the future with optimism. A few months later, the MD also resigned the management position and redeemed his shares at GV Victoria. I was appointed President of

---

12   National Hockey League (NHL)
13   Chief Executive Officer (CEO)

GV Victoria; the school's director would report directly to me as the board's representative. This was a role I was to hold for the next 16 years, keeping abreast of things from Calgary and mentoring different onsite directors. As of this writing, I am still involved with GV Victoria as the Board Chair.

It became apparent to those gathered for our May 2003 meeting that the Shane Global Village alliance would not survive 2004 but we felt that a second year was necessary. We knew that an immediate about-face would be even harder to explain in the market. As it turned out, there was no big rupture of the Shane Global Village partnership. The MD stepped down and by the time another meeting convened, it was clear that Global Village schools would go back to being just that for 2005. Shane English schools would also revert to how they were, marketing on their own. The school and marketing representatives of both sides of Global Village and Shane remained on good terms professionally and many had become friends.

After the Shane Global Village alliance ended, I decided I needed to take a more active role in the marketing of the GV Calgary and GV Victoria schools. GV Marketing would now be able focus on its five schools (four in Canada and one in the US) unencumbered. One of the advantages of the GV model was that school managers could focus on administration of the schools rather than participating in a lot of marketing trips. We relied on GVEC staff for that. One way in which GV school managers could support GV Marketing's efforts was by travelling now and then to key countries, which currently sent students, as well as to potential new source countries.
I believed in supporting GV Marketing's role more than just financially from the schools' budgets and looked for opportunities to develop and market the businesses of GV Calgary and GV Victoria from my base in Calgary.

I had the opportunity to fly to Europe for ten days in June 2003. David Antonisz was also a marketer in Europe with the SGV team. He told me that he was going to Sweden for three days and thought there might be some opportunities there for marketing the Canadian schools, especially for the less well-known destinations of Calgary and Victoria. Through this three-day adventure across Sweden, I gained a first-hand insight into the intense travel schedules of our marketing staff.

After a full day downtown at GV Calgary, I boarded an evening flight and washed up at Heathrow at about noon the next day. After catching a few hours of head-lolling sleep waiting in the airport, I flew to Copenhagen where I met David. We then boarded a ferry to Helsingborg in Sweden.

I became more aware that marketing staff who do these trips usually do not get the credit that should be their due. Sometimes staff back at schools greet them upon their return as if they have been on overseas holidays. The reality is that international business travel is often a real grind. On this trip, my empathy increased for our GV Marketing road warriors, some of whom spent more than 90 days a year away from home, making many personal and family sacrifices. Trips bring risks and not all marketing journeys bring results. That can be disheartening.

In Sweden, I had the international business traveller's experience of extreme jetlag mixed with negligible recovery time. I turned up at meetings feeling as if I had been cast in a zombie movie. In Helsingborg, even though I was exhausted, it took me hours to get to sleep in my room that seemed right out of an Ikea catalogue. When I finally nodded off, it seemed that David was on the phone five minutes later. Having missed meeting him in the hotel lobby at the appointed time, I scrambled to be on time for the meeting with an agent. Fortunately, I had employed the travelling marketer's tactic of shaving before I went to bed, and only unpacking a toothbrush, comb and what I needed to wear the next day.

As we journeyed by train across Sweden to Stockholm, David gave me insights into some European agencies. He related some of his hilarious experiences. On one occasion, he set out in a snowstorm to visit a Swiss agent in a town. David recalled that some kids even threw snowballs at him when he finally trudged up the street where the agent was located. When he knocked on the door, the agent swung the door open immediately and greeted him with the words, "You're late!"

We met with agents in the Stockholm harbour area and nearby in Uppsala, as well as at different locations where the train stopped on the way back to Malmo. The speed of moving from place to place and on one occasion meeting an agent near a statue in Stockholm Square added to the surreal nature of the trip. At times, I felt like we were in a European spy movie.

It turned out that there was little business opportunity for the schools in Canada. Swedish students had access to a European scholarship which enabled them to study English cheaply in the UK in the era long before anyone had heard of Brexit[14]. Agents were highly unlikely to encourage their clients to take on the much higher expense of travelling and studying in North America. Swedish agents asked me polite questions in their lilting English about Canada and there was a shared understanding about living in a liberal democracy in a northern climate. Sweden was also following the global trend of becoming increasingly multicultural.

In reflecting on this trip and approaches to marketing GV Calgary, I was reminded about how many players there are in helping a language program sustain business. Key variables include agent partners, who can be localized in the same city or scattered around the world, and the attitude of all staff to the mission of the school. I adopted the mantra that "Everyone's in marketing". When appropriate, I communicated to individuals and in staff meetings that all staff engagements with others, within the school and outside on activities and excursions, are on behalf of the business. They all count.

I noted, for example, that within the school, administrative staff

---

14 Brexit was the name given to the withdrawal of the United Kingdom from the European Union

and teachers could be co-operative partners in counselling students to make good decisions about future study plans. I clarified my expectations that teachers could also influence students to extend their enrollment in the school and could impact enrollment positively by welcoming visiting agents into their classrooms. At GV Calgary we encouraged staff to promote our own programs unashamedly because we believed in their worth to students. We also made the connection in staff meetings of the link between more students and being able to retain and hire more staff.

As the journey with Global Village continued and I gave the marketing of the Calgary and Victoria schools greater managerial attention, I got to know Robin Adams. Robin had been hired a few months earlier to work for GV Marketing and in August 2005 he was to head up the marketing of the five GV schools, as Cam Harvey was leaving. Cam had made a major contribution to Global Village in the ten years he worked with the schools.

In January 2006, Robin and I had a bonding experience on a marketing trip to Korea where we spent three days in the windblown, wintry streets of Seoul finding our way to meetings with agents. My time in Korea was brief and I was on my way back from down under again. Robin, though, had been putting in the hard yards for weeks, pounding pavement in meeting after meeting with a plethora of agents.

The meetings I attended were not without their humorous moments. Four of our partners claimed in separate meetings that they were each the number one agent in Korea. This reinforced the overall impression that South Korea was an extremely competitive, cut-throat, business-oriented country.

We took a cab to visit the gentleman who was in fact Global Village's number one agent, not only in Korea, but among all countries at the time, in terms of the registration of student weeks. Robin and I had a serious discussion about the commission increase this key agent was seeking. At the time, we were paying him 20 percent commission on tuition.

Robin advocated, "JT, he's going to expect 25 percent or we will lose him as an agent and a big chunk of market share."

"Where's it going to end, Robin? If we pay 25 percent, it's a slippery slope. Pretty soon, we will be paying 30 or even 35 percent", I replied.

"I know it's hard in a slim margin business, but can we afford to lose the business?" Robin asked.

I countered his question with a question, "Why is it that we always have to come up with an increase of 5 percent. Why can't we go for something like a 3 percent increase and offer 23 percent? Every percentage point or two that the school retains matters."

"We can try," said Robin wistfully.

The meeting with the agent went very well. Robin made a compelling case that, as part of our cost overhead, Global Village schools had to pay good teachers and other staff reasonable wages to maintain our high quality. We could not afford to pay as high commission as the chains and some other competitors. Robin maintained that we were the "no headache schools". When he pressed the point that our partners could have confidence in GV schools, that they would not receive complaints from their clients, and could therefore move on to their next sales, the agent nodded in agreement.

Even though I was in the choir that he was preaching to, I could see how lucky we were to have Robin heading our marketing team. We had the excellent fortune to have Robin leading GV Marketing for over 12 more years. The agent in this case accepted the increase to 23 percent. However, within two years, even quicker than I expected, his commission and that of other Korean partners had increased to 35 percent.

Robin and members of the GV Marketing team made regular trips to Korea, just as they did to other source countries for our students.

Along with school staff, such as registrars, we had to build and maintain relationships, and provide consistently high-quality service to agents and students. This paid off in terms of agents enrolling students. GV schools in Canada consistently had high Korean enrollment. In fact, in all but one month in 24 years at GV Calgary, Koreans had the strongest nationality representation in our school.

Our marketers did an excellent job in communicating with agents while Global Village was constantly changing the number of locations in its group between 1996 and 2008, especially in the alliance with Shane English Schools in 2003 and 2004.

Three Australian schools were promoted along with the five GV schools in North America under the Global Village brand after the SGV alliance ended. This included SGV Brisbane, which was started from scratch in 2003, along with the Sydney school with Mikio at the helm of both.

A new player and a new school entered the frame. Ian Pratt, a marketer in Japan with Shane English schools, and I met when he visited Calgary in May 2003. A quintessential Aussie and a graduate of an MBA[15] program, Ian was ambitious. He was also confident in his marketing skills, which were complemented by his Japanese language fluency. He had taken CELTA, so he was also aware of quality teaching practices.

In 2004, Ian presented the idea of adding a pre-existing school, Sunshine Coast English College in Noosa, to the Global Village group. He was buying most of the previous owner's shares, who would stay on as a minority shareholder. There was another small percentage of shares up for sale in the Noosa school. Cathie and I agreed to go in on this.

Noosa is a lovely area on the east coast of Australia. Located on the Sunshine Coast about 150 kilometres north of Brisbane in the state of Queensland, the area is not as well-known as the Gold Coast to the

---

15   Master of Business Administration (MBA)

south of Brisbane. The Noosa school had a lot of potential in a tropical seaside location. Ian was very motivated to make it a success.

Yet there were difficult discussions about the Australian schools' membership in the GV group and what they would pay as their share of marketing costs. These were worked out in three days of meetings in Toronto in December 2004, when all involved agreed that, at least for an interim period, the three schools of Sydney, Brisbane and Noosa would have associate membership status and be marketed as Global Village schools.

I flew to Brisbane from Toronto through Los Angeles, stopping for a few days in Sydney. Ian had asked me to come to Noosa for a week to meet with the teachers and advise on the management of the school. Some of the teachers were concerned about the vibe of a small school being upset by being part of the Global Village group. I noted again that change, even for the better, can be threatening.

Ian and I held a meeting with the teachers. I gave some background on Global Village and explained that the key goals were enrolling students and maintaining quality in teaching and related programs to sustain and develop the business. It was clear that there were dedicated teachers and administrative staff who could make the venture work.

After the teachers' meeting, one teacher came over to talk to me. She reported that most of the teachers, the silent majority, were glad to be part of Global Village. They saw opportunities for student enrollment to grow and for teachers to have more job security. Now we were getting somewhere. Ian deserves a lot of credit because he was able to increase the average enrollment in the school from 50 students to about 200 within about six months and the school went on to flourish.

My involvement in the Noosa school reminded me of how managers need to balance the dizzying array of day-to-day administration tasks of the school, especially in a start-up, relocation or new ownership phase. This often goes hand in hand with all the drama and expectations of an expanding agent and international student base, not to mention all the marketing energy expended to achieve that.

There was so much going in the Noosa school. We were lucky to have a mature and dedicated director of studies, who had worked for the original school owner. There was an experienced small administrative team as well as good teachers. At one stage, the Homestay Coordinator marched into Ian's office, almost out of breath. She was holding her mobile phone away from her ear and we could hear a woman's voice on the line. The staff person saw the funny side but wanted Ian and me to know about the woman's complaint and what she was dealing with. The complainant was a neighbour of one of the school's host families and exclaimed that when she looked out her window around midnight, "Two of YOUR students were fornicating under the bushes in MY front yard."

A more solvable problem was dealing with a teacher's concern that a giant cane toad, an infamous and ugly member of a species that had invaded Queensland, had found its way into a classroom.

Mikio and I persuaded Ian to become involved as an owner in Brisbane so that the business would do better. Ian agreed and put in place an excellent manager, who oversaw a lot of day-to-day management issues in Brisbane and Noosa while Ian paid particular attention to marketing, often travelling overseas.

Several years later, the Australian schools ended their alliance with Global Village. Their market focus was quite different from that of the GV schools in North America. It was also clear that Ian wished to leverage the GV brand and his arduous travel across the globe to recruit agent partners to form his own "Lexis" brand, which has since done very well. Mikio stayed involved with the schools in Sydney and Brisbane. It has always been a pleasure for me to see Mikio and Ian on different visits down under.

In 2014, after ten years' involvement as a partner, and with Cathie's encouragement, I simplified my life by selling our shares in the

Brisbane and Noosa schools. Ian and I sealed the deal by shaking hands in the shopping centre car park at Noosa Junction. It was a great relief. Now, I could concentrate on two schools in Canada.

Global Village Calgary and its sister schools in Hawaii, Toronto, Vancouver and Victoria flourished in the years after the alliances ended with the Shane English schools and the Australian schools. GV Marketing representatives emphasized our thriving locations and the strength of our programs. I listened and carefully considered what our marketers reported about what agents and students were looking for in language school experiences at our locations in Calgary and Victoria.

For years when competitors or agent partners would say to me that GV was not growing because it was not adding schools, I flinched at the implication that we were stagnating. I responded with words such as, "Please visit one of our locations, check out the cultural diversity and energy level, and talk to our students." It was always encouraging and affirming when an agent or delegation of agents visited one of our locations.

I highly valued the efforts of our Calgary-based agents and our international agent partners, especially when the latter took the time and made the effort to travel to Calgary. Most were impressed with the infrastructure and the feel of Calgary as a modern city with a population edging past 1.2 million in 2010.

In December of the same year, Igor, who represented a major Russian agency, visited Calgary during a day when we were hit by a raging blizzard. We had snowstorms in Calgary, of course, but remarkably few that interrupted our business. As Igor and I made our way around snowbanks, slipping down icy streets in downtown Calgary and riding the light rail transit train up the hill to visit the Southern Alberta Institute of Technology (SAIT), he joked, "Calgary is just like Moscow. I can sell this!"

TIPS

If you are a teacher or an administrative staff member:

- Recognize and support the role and efforts of marketing staff
- Consider ways in which you can promote the school in your interaction with students
- Be willing to meet visiting agents to the school and allow them to sit in on classes

If you are a manager:

- Recognize and support the role and efforts of marketing staff
- Think carefully about the branding identity of your school and influence it positively
- Consider the relative weight of priority to give to administration and marketing in the business's annual life cycle and overall trajectory
- Seek new business opportunities while maintaining the core of the business
- Cultivate productive working partnerships with local, national and international agent partners
- Utilize opportunities to showcase your city and school or program
- Enjoy the places you visit and the international cast of characters whom you meet in the language business

Global Citizens

On March 17, 2009 George W. Bush was giving a speech in Calgary. It was his first speech to an audience as the ex-President of the United States. Calgary professionals in the oil and gas industry gave the controversial Mr. Bush a respectful hearing when he spoke at the Calgary Convention Centre, just two blocks from Global Village Calgary.

I had not registered that George Bush was speaking nearby, when I took a brief noon-hour walk down Stephen Avenue. There was an exceptionally large cardboard cutout of Bush displayed outside the Convention Centre. It was piled high with shoes.

George W. Bush had famously dodged two shoes thrown at him in protest at a Baghdad press conference in December 2008, a month before his presidency ended. With the Bush visit to Calgary, a local charitable organization had crafted the effigy of Bush as a light-hearted way for people to protest Bush's policies, with the intention of donating the shoes to people living in poverty or on the streets.

As I made my way back to the school, I heard sirens blaring and Bush's motorcade rolled quickly past. In one fleeting moment, I was standing on a street corner looking directly at Bush. He was smiling back at me through the window of his limo in a way that was eerily reminiscent of Maxwell Smart, the bumbling spy character in the 1960s spoof, *Get Smart*[16]. In an instant George W. Bush was gone. I did not even have enough time to remove and throw my shoes at him!

As I continued my walk, I considered this brief synchronicity of one of the world's most influential leaders of the first decade of the 21st century intersecting with where I was at a certain time and

---

16   *Get Smart*, American TV series (1965-70)

place. I also reflected on the clever opportunism of the organization supporting people who suffer from poverty, even in a comparatively wealthy city like Calgary. Its efforts in highlighting and trying to address in a small way, an issue that is very real to a lot of people, reminded me again of how we are connected to others.

Life with its rhythm and challenges continues. In the day-to-day life of a language program, we find it easy to get caught up in the human drama that goes with being in a people-focussed business. Sometimes it seems that we are operating in wave after wave of extenuating circumstances. It might seem obvious, but we need to remind ourselves that what happens inside a business is also related to the social, economic and cultural contexts of our times and locations.

When I managed language programs, I was compelled to consider responses and practical strategies that would promote a culture where colleagues and the organization itself could prove resilient in times of adversity. With the luxury of hindsight, I can reflect on many challenging times both as a teacher and a manager when I had to work out appropriate responses to the stress of others, including to students in distress or even sometimes acting out. Like everyone else, I also had to deal with my own stress.

Things that go on in the world, as well as in our students' and our own lives, colour our perspectives. When I was an ESL instructor at Mount Royal College[17] in the late 1980s, several incidents in class showed that the students' thoughts of home were never far from their minds. One day, there was a loud honking of horns on the street outside the downtown campus. "Pinochet is dead," joked the student from Chile.

There were also four Nicaraguan students in the class. Three of them hung out together and the other, an older guy with a military bearing, kept to himself. One day I quietly asked one in the group of three why they didn't mix with the older gentleman.

---

17 Now called Mount Royal University

"Because he's a Contra!" she hissed.

Students' stories prompted me to give more consideration to my interactions. I learned to be more sensitive to students, based on what might have happened to them. One day, as I introduced a reading about earthquakes to a Mount Royal class, I tried to draw students into the lesson by asking if they had ever experienced an earthquake. After a few minutes, I noticed a student quietly weeping at the back of the classroom. At the break, she told me that a relative had died in a recent earthquake in Japan. She apologized for crying. I told her that it was me who had to apologize.

Events in the world influenced my thinking about my role as a teacher and later when I became a manager. Soon after we moved to Lethbridge, a pall seemed to hang over the university. The Montréal massacre on December 6, 1989, when a gunman walked into a university engineering class at École Polytechnique and killed fourteen female students in a targeted misogynistic slaying, deeply shocked people in Canada. In educational settings, we increased our attention to student and staff safety. We reflected on how relationships among men and women could work better in society as a whole and in the spheres where we had influence.

In my managerial positions, I worked with others to try to build environments where people would relate and work well together. When we opened GV Calgary in 1996, it was only a little over four years since the massive media coverage accorded the all-white male US Senate Judiciary Committee hearing of Anita Hill's allegations of sexual harassment against Clarence Thomas. Despite the riveting testimony, Clarence Thomas was appointed and still sits as a judge on the US Supreme Court.

At the time, institutions were examining and reframing their policies to prevent sexual harassment. There was a movement afoot to clarify expectations for relationships in workplaces and to deal with possible complaints and sanctions. The *Me Too* movement of recent years has underscored that businesses and individuals need to be more than just mindful of the way people interact, and address how we behave.

At Global Village, we were adamant about running schools where all people felt safe and valued. Our policies were intended to move beyond mere rhetoric or guidelines. Every day was an exercise in living up to these expectations.

We recognized that change is constant in life and in language programs and that world events have a great influence on business. As in all walks of life, so many forces set the context of managing a business. For example, economic factors cause currency fluctuations, which influence where students can afford to travel abroad. Upheavals in the world like 9/11 and the pandemic are socio-political realities that impact us all. We were forced again and again to respond both individually and collectively, amid the tremors of change, to people we served and to others we worked alongside.

Challenges continued to roll in. As the end of 1999 approached, it was Y2K[18] that was on everyone's list. From the vantage point of over twenty years later, it is curious to reflect that the concern with how computer systems would handle the time signature of ticking over at midnight into January 1, 2000 would be such an issue.

In early December 1999 we had approximately 200 students. 30 students (or 15 percent of the overall school population) were from Venezuela. This was the highest number of Venezuelan students who attended GV Calgary at one time. Calgary and Caracas had good business and flight connections because of the oil industry. But the dramatic and sad political upheavals in Venezuela over the subsequent years greatly reduced the representation of the popular and friendly Venezuelan students in our school.

We also had a serious downturn in enrollment just prior to December 31, 1999. Almost all the Latin American students left before we would see if Y2K was going to be a factor or simply a

---

18 Year 2000 (Y2K)

myth. Along with many other students, we concluded that they or their parents worried that the lights would go out in Calgary and that we would be plunged into freezing darkness if the city's infrastructure was not able to cope.

This combined with the normal winter attrition in enrollment, which the school experienced every year over the Christmas and New Year period. GV Calgary's population plummeted to under 100 students, the lowest it had been since the first three months of the school in 1996. It represented a harbinger of what was to come many years later when the pandemic hit in 2020.

Another challenge arose locally. In early February 2001, I returned from a family holiday in Australia to the harshness of the Canadian winter and the problems caused by a seven-week-long Calgary transit strike. At the same time, Vancouver was also experiencing a lengthy strike by transit workers. The Manager of GV Vancouver worked out a schedule with an independent bus company. Students would be picked up at various points around the city of Vancouver and taken to and from the school. Students covered the costs by each paying a fare.

This strategy was not going to work in Calgary, in my view. Our homestays were spread out across the city. There simply were no companies with any extra buses available. I tried to see if host families would volunteer to ferry their students and get involved in car-pooling. But host families were dealing with their own commuting challenges. Those hosts who were available to run a pick-up service wanted to be paid, at least to cover their gas costs and their time. They recognized that GV Calgary was a profit-making entity. Understandably, they did not wish to offer their services for free.

Concerned about losing the student base, I hurriedly put a system in place which involved paying a select number of host families an honorarium for driving students back and forth to the school. Perhaps I should have communicated that more clearly to the Global Village Managing Director. Yet I was concerned that he did not understand the Calgary context. I correctly anticipated being questioned about why I was not doing the same thing as GV Vancouver. In managing the crisis, I did what I thought was best; however, it was a controversial decision within the organization.

When the transit strike finally ended, and the bill for honorariums was tabulated at $10,000, the Managing Director criticized me by email and at a board meeting. I stood my ground. I thought the solution was the only workable option open to us in Calgary. I also thought it was a reasonable price to pay, as we did not lose students. Unlike in temperate Vancouver, Calgary students were not going to either wait or walk distances in the crushing cold.

As managers in business or just as a natural human reaction, people feel the stress keenly when a situation lands squarely on them. When they try to deal with a crisis in a logical way, when there are limited options available, and especially when the choices they made prove effective, it feels like naysayers are piling on.

I worked hard to manage my stress, and I had support at home. I used walking to the school and back each day as therapy while public transit was not running. Even though Cathie was busy completing her doctorate degree in community health sciences, she continued to shoulder more than her share of family responsibilities by getting the boys up and ready for school, so I could head out early each day.

I devised a one-hour walking route where I could cut across country from my home and walk into the heart of Calgary along the Bow River, which was partially frozen. On most mornings, the temperature was well below freezing. Condensation wafted like smoky tendrils across the Bow River Valley. While I enjoyed the calm of chilly winter mornings, I projected my thoughts onto the environment which looked to me like it was blowing off steam.

We soon found out that a local transit disruption paled in comparison to events on September 11, 2001. It is now a cliché to ask where you were on 9/11. At least once in a generation, a tectonic event like the assassination of John F. Kennedy in 1963, or the atomic bombings of Hiroshima and Nagasaki in 1945, rocks the world to its core. People think about where they were at the time of such events, both in terms of physical location and what they were doing in their lives.

On September 11, 2001, I was taking a mental health day. Before I went for a morning swim, CBC[19] News had a newsflash about a plane that had crashed into the World Trade Centre in New York. An hour later when I got back in my car and listened to the radio for an update, all hell had broken loose. When I arrived home, our son John George, who was 15 at the time, called out that another plane had crashed into the World Trade Centre.

Cathie, John and I watched the television updates in real time as the second tower crumbled to the ground. It was unbelievable. We continued with the daily aspects of our family routines. I drove John to and from soccer practice and picked up David, our younger son who was then six, from after-school childcare. All the while, the news streamed in about the scope of the terrorist attack and the dislocation caused. For a while, the whereabouts of the President of the United States, George W. Bush, was unknown. It turned out that he had been whisked away in Air Force One, incommunicado, and surrounded by fighter jets.

On September 12, I caught the light rail transit train as usual. Not a word was spoken in a train carriage full of commuters into the downtown core of Calgary. It was preternaturally quiet as we were all lost in our own thoughts. Everyone seemed in shock at the events of the day before.

Our Activities Coordinator had arranged a hike in the Rockies for a group of students on the following Saturday. He did not want to go. Most of the students had also pulled out but three Japanese women had their hearts set on the day out. It was possibly the only time they might have the opportunity to go hiking in the Rocky Mountains in Canada.

---

19   Canadian Broadcasting Corporation (CBC)

I decided to take the students out for the hike. It was a perfect fall day with an azure blue sky clear of any clouds. The leaves on the trees were in their spectacular stage of turning a rich variety of colours. We ended up hiking 19 kilometres up to the waterfalls and back along Ribbon Creek in Kananaskis Country, a provincial recreation area on the east side of the Rockies about 100 kilometres west of Calgary. We followed the gently undulating trail beside the creek, which flowed quietly. The exercise and trickling sound of the water running was soothing in the pristine serenity of the mountains.

One of the students, Chieko, emailed me upon her return to Japan and told me how much the day meant to her. She was from Okinawa and had met another student from her home island at GV Calgary. In Japan, their friendship continued to blossom as they decided to share an apartment while they explored job prospects in Tokyo. Hearing such an affirming story lifted my spirits.

At the time, I was worn down by the relentless business of managing Global Village Calgary and working within a centralized administration system based in Vancouver. I was determined that this dark period in my professional life was not going to affect my outlook in the school or in my family relationships.

When facing criticism or hard times, as difficult as they were, I found the best way forward was often just to hang tough and to look for joy with my family and other pursuits. I discovered anew that learning opportunities lay among the negatives. Focussing on the positives, which were there if I looked hard enough for them, helped immensely.

I decided to stay on board with Global Village to see where the journey would take me. In October 2001, I had the opportunity to return to Hokkaido in Japan for ten days. Since travelling with the University of Lethbridge student groups in 1991 and 1993, I had also returned to Hokkaido in 1998 on a marketing trip.

As I had done in 1998, I took a train through the picturesque mountains in Hokkaido from Sapporo to Obihiro. The Japanese people, whom I knew, said that they were reeling from 9/11, which recalled for many the national trauma that occurred in 1945 and the period around then. They welcomed me and said travelling internationally again so soon after the event was a positive step.

Hisashi Urashima, whom had I met many years before, owned and operated an English school there. I promoted Global Village at a one-day marketing event at his Joy English Academy. Urashima-san, who looked like a Japanese version of Canadian singer-songwriter Bruce Cockburn, told me how and why he started his English school. He said that many years before he had enjoyed a year studying English as an exchange student in the United States. He observed that back in Japan in the 1980s, however, learning English for most Japanese was not fun and more like drudgery. Breaking free of his life as a salaryman[20], he started his own school in his small home city of Obihiro, surrounded by bucolic countryside. He called his school Joy English Academy because he wanted learning English to be as positive for students as it had been for him.

I revelled in hearing such stories. I learned more about cultural perspectives in Japan on each of my adventures there. I loved their sensibilities for art and nature. I delighted in the dry humour of Japanese people I met, both when I was in Japan and when they were students in Canada.

Hearing their stories was fuel to the fire of my intercultural interests and gave me fresh perspective in reflecting on events in the world and in my work. My four trips to Japan, especially the one I made in the fall of 2001, allowed me to catch my career breath. It renewed my optimism and sense of purpose for working in the language business. Challenges were not going to disappear, but I felt that these journeys helped me build up experience and stamina to approach them pragmatically.

Another impactful event was just around the corner for us in Calgary. In June 2002, the G8 Conference was held in Kananaskis

---

20 Salaryman means a white-collar worker, especially in Japan.

Country. Because 9/11 was fresh in everyone's minds, security was paramount. Even though the conference was deliberately planned to be held outside the city so that a defence perimeter could be maintained, the City of Calgary was placed on full alert.

Security precautions were ramped up. We had to do a full-scale evacuation drill, this time orchestrated by the management of Gulf Canada Square and police authorities, and not prompted by one of our students, as had occurred several years earlier. As the manager, I was told in advance that when the alarm sounded, the school was not to give any indication that it was a drill. Officials wanted this to be treated very seriously.

One afternoon in early June, Gulf Canada Square was completely emptied out for an hour by an evacuation order. We had to walk with staff and about 200 students, all the way down nine floors of stairs and onto the railway tracks that run behind Gulf Canada Square. It remains a peculiarity of Calgary and many other Canadian cities that the Canadian Pacific Railway, built more than one hundred years ago to open up Western Canada, still actually runs through the core of the central business district.

Some students were not pleased with this security exercise. When it was over, I found two mature Brazilian students waiting outside my office. They complained bitterly about the lack of warning and protested that they had been extremely frightened by the evacuation. They told me they had friends who had been killed in one of the World Trade Centre buildings in New York on 9/11. I told them I was deeply sorry about their friends. I explained the context of the drill and that the school had been told not to give a warning. They were only partially placated.

Clearly, we all continue to be impacted by world events. It is understandable that we might be tempted to wring our hands about global prospects for the future as the weight of events such as climate change, global pandemics, wars and massive dislocations of people bear down. However, I firmly believe that the act of people travelling for language study and understanding other cultures casts a ray of light. I am not suggesting that international education is a panacea for the world's problems but it provides a hopeful touchstone. Who can deny that we all could use a little hope?

TIPS

If you are a teacher:

- Recognize that events in the world impact your life and your students' lives
- Welcome opportunities to engage in topics related to current affairs
- Understand that students may want your perspectives to help make sense of their experiences in a new country
- Be especially sensitive to students' backgrounds and cultural nuances in discussion of topics

If you are a manager:

- All the above, and
- Be clear in your communication and your decision-making in escalating situations
- Be prepared to be misunderstood and be able to defend your decisions
- Manage your stress by breaks, exercise and being kind to yourself in reflecting on decisions
- Look for opportunities to refresh your career

Buckle up!

Life in the language industry is full of ups and downs. In my experience that is just how it is. During any period of turbulence, like an air traveller on a bumpy flight, I tried just to buckle up and stoically ride it out. We learned the hard way that stress triggers for those of us working in language programs can range across a whole host of factors from seismic global events, the policies of different governments and disasters like a flood to even one student acting out.

The school was again busy in the heat of the Calgary summer in July 2012. One day, I was late for work and furiously cycled the twenty minutes from home to school. As there always seemed to be, there was one student who had been leading us a merry dance. As I got closer to the school, there he was, leaning on the outside of the front door. Dressed in his distinctive all-green clothes and the beginnings of dreadlocks with loud, hip-hop music oozing from his headphones, he was grooving to his own vibe, while insouciantly toking on a joint.

This was over six years before marijuana was legalized in Canada. The student, who was from Saudi Arabia, blew me off when I told him that what he was doing was inappropriate. I came on too strong. The student slumped away scowling. His high had turned into a low for both of us.

A recent communique from the Saudi Arabian Cultural Bureau, which funded students in language programs, had suggested that language schools and programs should report back to them about their students who were not conforming to the traditional norms of Saudi culture. I was reluctant to be a part of this Orwellian oversight but in my frustration with the student, I decided to test the waters with a softened approach.

I cloaked an enquiry about the student's study status to the Bureau in general concerns about his not following school attendance rules or Canadian social norms. I did not call him out to the Bureau on his love for the "evil weed". The following day, the student came storming into my office. Now he was anything but the "cool dude". The Bureau had contacted him directly, leaving me out of the loop.

He asked angrily, "Why did you call the Bureau?"

He got more worked up, even after I asked him to relax and offered him a seat. I pointed out that I wanted him to have a wake-up call, which he reported to have received. Ironically, the Bureau had evidently called before his normal waking hour which was after morning classes began. Very calmly, I told him that he was very bright and capable of achieving a degree but that he was wasting his time in Canada. He said that he did not want to be at Global Village but wanted to be at the University of Calgary.

With my tongue not too firmly embedded in my cheek, I persuaded him that this might indeed be a better fit for him than "studying" at GV. I encouraged him to take the ESL program at the University of Calgary to qualify for entrance to a degree program. He took my advice and we officially parted ways.

I like to think he went on to become a successful student and global citizen when he returned to his own society. Earning degrees was the whole raison d'etre for the Saudi Government's King Abdullah School Scholarship Program. It was designed to help students earn degrees in other countries and contribute their expertise in Saudi Arabia. I have no idea if that happened. So often this is the case with international students because we lose touch after they leave.

Fortunately, we had not come to depend on Saudi students at GV Calgary in the way that many private and public sector programs had across Canada. Their enrollment numbers took a serious hit in August 2018 when the Canadian politician and current Deputy Prime Minister Chrystia Freeland tweeted about human rights abuses by the Saudi Government. The Saudis took great exception to the tweet.

This became a full-scale international incident. Thousands of Saudi students were forced to interrupt their studies in Canada and return home. The students, as well as language and university programs across Canada, were forced to adapt. The Saudi Government backed down a few months later but only after a huge amount of dislocation, much of which could not be readily remediated.

As we approached the summer of 2013 at Global Village Calgary, I might have been forgiven for thinking that, despite all the ongoing challenges, we were doing well, and this would continue for a while at least. We had negotiated a five-year extension on our original ten-year lease for the building we were in. We had an excellent team of administrative staff and teachers, with minimal turnover. Language program enrollment and IELTS candidate numbers were up.

But life in the language industry reflects life in general. Unprecedented events can strike without warning and disrupt all equilibrium and plans. In the third week of June, what started as a seemingly innocuous rainstorm intensified. A low-pressure front settled over the Rockies and would not shift.

The rain started in earnest on a Thursday, bucketing down in an inundation of biblical proportions. By Friday morning, the Bow River, overwhelmed from both the rain and the thawing runoff from snow in the adjacent Rockies, was overflowing the streets of downtown Calgary. GV Calgary was only two blocks from the river and because a lot of the electrical infrastructure was underground in our area, power was quickly cut off to our building. It was breathtaking how suddenly a flood emergency transpired in Calgary.

While riding my bike from home to school, I traversed roads which were becoming small rivers. The fast-flowing Bow River was running almost up to the bottom of the Peace Bridge. Memorial Drive was closed to traffic and covered in muddy water. On Friday, the students and staff who had turned up at the school could not go indoors for their classes. We sent them home with directions to stay safe and to check for messages on the school's website and twitter platforms. Rain continued steadily over the weekend. The city was in a state of emergency.

It was the last week of June and we were preparing for our largest intake of new students for the year. We scrambled. We had 250 students registered. Within a week we expected this number to rise to over 300 and we had nowhere to hold classes. Authorities recommended that people stay away from areas of Calgary's downtown core where the power was cut off. But in true Canadian fashion, this was advised rather than enforced, so we pressed on.

Each morning, teachers met students in the park across from the school and conducted classes in local coffee shops and nearby public parks. Our administrative team rustled up the school's main computers and set up a command centre at the home of Carla and Terry, our Head Registrar and Director of Programs. While cycling to work, I cast anxious looks at the roiling river and the flooded streets near the school.

The interior of the school was in darkness. Staff and students continued to adapt. I got to know a Colombian student in his late sixties who had a bladder issue. Every morning I led him by flashlight to a washroom in the dark, empty school. I accepted that helping him out was all part of my morning routine in that week of upheaval. Sometimes it is better to help solve a simple problem, rather than fuming about the added burden amid the chaos. Small victories count in the face of a major crisis.

One two-part question hung in the air. When would the power be back on in our section of the city and when could we reopen? All other areas of the city were back on the power grid, but not ours. I directed questions to the over-taxed City of Calgary officials, the local member of parliament and the head of the management company for our building, without satisfaction. The building manager lectured me about what I already knew and rebuffed my attempts to lobby for the welfare of the school's business. It was true that people were losing their homes, jobs and businesses due to the flood. However, I held my ground in pointing out that the whole enterprise of the school and many GV Calgary jobs were also at risk if this situation were to continue much longer.

After a week of swimming in chaos and doubt, we came to the final Friday of the month. Every fourth Friday, teachers distributed monthly progress assessment reports to the students and there was always a group of students leaving. We carried on and held a brief graduation at the Globe Cinema in the downtown core as per usual. We still had no idea where we would be on Monday.

Agents and students had been contacting us all week from across the world asking if those registered for classes in July should still come. These enquiries were echoed by my niece, Amanda, who was travelling from Australia and visiting relatives in the United States. She was an ESL teacher in training and planned to come to stay with us for six weeks, so she could work with the summer teen program.

We told all our students and staff, as well as Amanda, that the show would go on. We continued to adapt. Administrative staff and teachers did a stellar job in banding together to keep programs running. Tania and Terry, with their positive "everything will be all right" attitudes, were great managers in the crisis. The IT[21] engine for the business kept running. The administrative team stayed focussed. The lines of communication remained open with our stakeholders and with each other.

We added some field trips to the itinerant class routine, but we sensed we could not sustain the students' patience for much longer. Fortunately, after a week we were getting subtle signals that the power problems could be resolved shortly. The power grid in our quadrant of downtown was back in operation and city crews were going from building to building to check them and to turn the power back on.

---

21 Information Technology (IT)

After eight days, the power was finally switched back on. We were given the go-ahead to open again for the busiest week of the year. What a relief! I gratefully reached for my sunglasses as the sun finally shone after all the rain. We had gained a huge reprieve to be able to re-open for classes.

I drove with Cathie to meet Amanda at the airport. We settled back for the weekend. Calgary felt like it was in a different country. The heat along with receding floodwaters left an unusual level of humidity. We sweltered in the tropical conditions of 33 degrees Celsius and over 90 percent humidity. We took our 21-year-old niece out for ice cream. Amanda said, "It's so hot. I did not expect it to be like this."

This was ironic coming from someone who lived in Australia. Making that point, I smilingly added, "Congratulations, Amanda. I've lived in Calgary and Alberta for almost 30 years and you've managed to arrive on the hottest, most humid day in all that time."

As 2013 progressed, we had a bumper number of candidates taking the IELTS test. The Alberta Government was encouraging the inflow of more "temporary foreign workers" who needed to pass IELTS to demonstrate a reasonable level of English proficiency. As well as GV Calgary's regular Saturday testing for over 200 students, we ran extra tests for over 300 candidates at the University of Calgary once a month from July through November.

Tania was doing superb work with her IELTS team. But because of just one Saturday's closure during the flood, testing had to be re-scheduled. It took us three months to deal with the backlog. The good news was that at the annual IDP/ IELTS Australia Conference, Tania accepted an award on behalf of GV Calgary for "outstanding performance as a centre in the face of extenuating circumstances". We were delighted that all the extra work was recognized. Tania totally deserved the credit for her leadership, although she noted to me that another nominee for the award was an IELTS centre in Tehran. They had run a test as Iranian protesters raged against their government outside their location. Shots had been fired. Tania thought they may have been more deserving.

TIPS

If you are a teacher or an administrative staff member:

- Recognize the context of problem students or serious events
- Use whatever influence you have judiciously
- Stay calm and carry on

If you are a manager:

- All the above, plus
- Be prepared to be challenged by difficult people and events
- Maintain your focus on key priorities
- Collaborate with key team members to put a crisis management strategy in place
- Consider other steps to develop "organizational resilience" with colleagues and your programs
- Communicate with stakeholders like students, marketing staff, host families and agent partners throughout an emergency

wellness and safety

In my experience, both firsthand and from what I've been told by colleagues over the years, most students report that they have positive experiences when they travel internationally for language study. However, some are distressed, often silently, in the upheaval caused by being out of the comfort zones of their own countries. Furthermore, students might be experiencing serious trauma, through no fault of their own or that of the institution.

Mental and physical health, which can be related to perceptions of individual safety, can become issues for all involved with a student in distress. In my opinion, managers are well advised to consider policies and actions that engage students and staff in wellness and safety practices as a core priority.

Regrettably, in the early years of Global Village (GV) Calgary, we enrolled a small number of students who were already in distress before they arrived as students. I have never understood the attitude of parents who encourage their children (of any age) to travel overseas to study when they are already not faring well at home. Being cast into an unfamiliar culture and unable to function properly speaking a new language is daunting for anyone. Yet for those who are already struggling with mental or physical problems, it can be truly terrifying.

A few students exhibited clear signs that they were unwilling or reluctant to leave home. They were sent anyway, into our care. In our first summer of 1996 at GV Calgary, we had a French 16-year-old who was more than homesick. He was almost catatonic in class and refused to engage with the teacher and his classmates. The host family also reported that they just could not relate to him because he stayed in his room all the time.

One day, a teacher reported that the student had drawn a picture of himself jumping off the Calgary Tower. It was a cry for help. I contacted a friend of mine, a suicide prevention counsellor. She confirmed that the student needed immediate professional intervention and gave me the name of community agencies to contact. The student, though, just wanted to go home to France. Lynn contacted the teenager's father, whose response was disturbing. He asked, "Why are you contacting me? My son is your problem. He will stay with you."

Lynn and I decided, without delay, to arrange for him to travel home. Lynn's next phone call to the father was brief, "Monsieur, your son will be arriving back in France," and he gave the time of arrival and flight number. We gave the student a full refund, less the change fee for the return airfare. Lynn accompanied the student to the airport. Later, he commented that the teenager was smiling for the first time that he could recall.

Just like other language schools and programs, GV Calgary unwittingly accepted students whose self-care should have come first, before studying overseas. One young woman from Switzerland turned out to be suffering from bulimia. After a brief time with us, she returned home. The stress of being an international student overwhelmed her.

In another incredibly sad case, a Latin American student in his 30s had to be admitted to the psychiatric ward at Foothills Hospital, Calgary. His obsessive-compulsive disorder was triggered, he became manic and was assessed as a possible suicide risk. How alienating it must have been for the student in his condition to be so far from home and his support network, in a totally unfamiliar city.

Once we thought that the student was safely looked after at the hospital, a nurse called to ask if he was back in class.

I fielded the call. "No, the student is not with us. Isn't he with you, at the Foothills?"

"Well, the thing is, he somehow got out of our secure facility and we don't know where he is." she said.

Rather than deconstructing the term "secure facility", our duty of care for the student became paramount when our receptionist came flapping into my office to tell me that someone from Calgary Airport had also just called. The student had turned up at the airport, in his pajamas no less, and wanted to purchase a ticket to fly back to his country.

We arranged for the hospital to send someone out to the airport to collect him while we contemplated further steps. When we had first become aware of the seriousness of his condition, we contacted the student's agent and said that we had not been informed on the application that the student had a mental health condition. We then asked the agent to arrange for a family member to travel to Calgary to be with him and to accompany him home when he was deemed fit to travel.

A few days after the shenanigans at the airport, the student's mother turned up at the school. It was a difficult and outlandish conversation, as she angrily accused the school's staff of treating her son unfairly. She went as far as saying that we had stolen money from him. Fortunately, I had been informed of some relevant facts, so was able to respond with a bit of background.

For a school event the week before, our Activities Coordinator had organized a group to attend a Calgary Flames hockey game. While our coordinator was sitting high up in the stands in the cheap seats ("the nosebleeds" as they are referred to because of their altitude and distance from the ice), he spotted our troubled Latin American student with six other students sitting right next to ice level, in the expensive section. It turned out that our Latin American student had paid for all those seats.

After I had told his mother, I struggled to maintain an even tone when she insisted that the school refund all the money that he had spent in Calgary. So, I carefully listed all the steps that staff at Global Village Calgary had taken to assist her son. She did concede that he had a "maníaco depresivo" (manic depressive or obsessive compulsive) condition but maintained that she thought he was all right to study abroad. I had to tell her that we had not been informed of his condition. Furthermore, I suggested that it was a serious misjudgement to think he could cope with studying abroad in such a different culture from his home.

The meeting remained tense. I tried to find some common ground with the student's mother. I said that I could not imagine her suffering, knowing what her son was experiencing. Left unsaid were the arguments and questions that I could imagine. It seemed possible to me that in her desperation, she had condoned or actively influenced the terrible decision for her son to study in Calgary. But that line of thinking was not productive. I knew that we needed to deal with the problem immediately. It took a bit of listening and calming, but in the end we agreed to get her son home as soon and as safely as possible.

As a result of a handful of such disturbing and sobering incidents, Global Village schools developed specific questions on the registration forms to prompt disclosure of any physical and mental conditions, in confidence and mindful of our duty of care. Still, mental health issues were not always disclosed and schools were left to puzzle them out, pick up the pieces and help in any way possible.

I am pleased that in recent years more credence has been given to the need to deal with the complicated issues of wellness for both staff and students. The topic of mental health and various supports for international students is now a regular subject for presentation and discussion at the annual Languages Canada Conference.

Over the years at GV Calgary, we have also had some extremely resilient and adventurous students who informed us up front that they had physical challenges. A student from Belgium had been blinded several years before arriving in Calgary. We were able to access support for her from the Canadian National Institute for the Blind.

We found that the whole school community rallied around such extraordinary students. On another occasion, a Korean student wrote on his registration form that his face was severely disfigured because of a fire several years before. He was determined to travel and study abroad. He attached a letter in which he noted that he had been working on his English, partially as therapy, and asked politely if he could come to Global Village Calgary.

When he arrived, his English was already at a high level. He had an amazingly gregarious personality. He made friends with all his classmates and mixed with students of every culture across the whole school. At our monthly graduation event, Global Village schools awarded Student of the Month to recognize the efforts of a student who had made extra-special efforts in the community of the school, in their learning and their participation in activities. When the Korean student received a Student of the Month award, the whole school assembly stood as one and clapped and cheered for minutes. In response, he gave a moving speech about the friends he had made in Calgary and what the experience had meant for him. There was not a dry eye in the place.

The disclosure of special needs by students on their registration applications allowed us to provide the necessary support on many occasions at GV Calgary. We also needed to be watchful and understanding of our teachers and staff. Most often they are not professionally-trained counsellors. So, we invited discussion of serious problems with senior managers. Together, it was possible to assess the situations, develop some clarity and decide what next steps might be. Sometimes students required help from outside professionals and it became the work of managers to facilitate that process.

On one occasion, our Director of Programs found out weeks after the fact that a recent graduate of our CELTA teacher training program was in over her head. It happened in the first class she taught for us. In this case, a female student misread the young teacher's caring nature as a romantic interest. She projected her own feelings onto the teacher by writing notes and talking to her after class. The teacher, who was recently married, found that the class was disrupted by this misunderstanding. She endured a huge amount of stress by not reaching out earlier to senior staff. After a conversation with the Director of Studies, the student was moved to another class.

Global Village Calgary, like most language schools and programs, took its duty of care for students seriously. We understand that students, who are far from home, take brave steps to leave their countries for a while and travel for language and cultural immersion in different countries. It often takes them way out of their comfort zone. Despite all the steps we put in place for orienting students to safety and ensuring criminal record checks of host families of students, the reality is that students face risks, as we all do.

The description that follows might be confronting for some readers, so I advise caution. Some may want to skip ahead to the last two paragraphs at the end of the chapter. Yet, among the overarchingly positive factors of an international study experience for most students, I feel it is important to recognize that language businesses are not immune from the worst of society.

Young people can be especially vulnerable, even in a relatively safe Canadian city like Calgary. Any crime against a person is reprehensible. We sometimes forget the sheer scope of individual hardship in the daily avalanche of news about massive human distress in all kinds of forms. Still, when there is someone in your own orbit who becomes a victim, such as a student at your school, it is like a thunderbolt striking close to home.

A 22-year-old student at GV Calgary reported to her teacher that she had been brutally plucked off the sidewalk by two young men in a van while walking home in the dark one evening in February 2014. They had each proceeded to rape her over several hours before letting her go.

The student's teacher told Tania and me about the assault. We were badly shaken. We wanted to support the student in the best way possible. The teacher was a pillar of strength to the student, and encouraged her to give a statement to the police. We arranged for a Calgary police officer to come to my office.

The student asked if the teacher and I could be present while she gave her statement to the male police officer. She gave her harrowing account, clutching tissues and crying uncontrollably at times. However, she gathered herself together and stated clearly what had happened to her. She noted that when the two men let her go, she was beyond relieved because she had feared for her life. She was drained by retelling and thus reliving her shocking experience.

The policeman remained matter of fact. Although the officer was sympathetic, it seemed he was merely going through the motions. As the police officer took the student's statement, the question ran through my mind about whether this would lead to any real investigation and possible arrests. After the teacher had led the student away to comfort her, I gave voice to my thought. The police officer responded that he would investigate the matter. Yet he admitted that he did not hold out great hope of catching the culprits.

I was dismayed by his apparent nonchalance. Even though I understood that the resources of police are stretched and they have many serious crimes to deal with, our student was the victim of a sexual assault. On any level this was an outrage. I insisted that the police should do more. I pressed the case on numerous subsequent occasions by calling the Calgary Police Service and quoting the case number. I was infuriated that I never got a call back. I still wonder if I should have done more at the time.

This crime greatly upset the small circle of school people who knew about it. We preserved the student's privacy. We were promoting Calgary as a safe destination and yet one of our students had been brutally raped and had been in fear for her life. The main thing was to focus on her welfare. The teacher continued to provide care and she encouraged, but did not press, the student into receiving counselling through various community crisis agencies. Surprisingly, the student extended her stay in Calgary and continued classes at GV. This seemed to exemplify that she found that the school community supported her.

Those of us in the know were hollowed out by thoughts of the student's experience. I was extremely worried that others in Calgary, possibly other international students, could also be victims of criminals. I thought a lot about what we in the language industry could do to protect our students.

As a co-chair of the Conference Committee for Languages Canada (LC), I worked with others to focus more on student safety and welfare. Issues surrounding the physical and mental wellness of international students are a growing concern and deserve more attention. I am comforted a little by the fact that the LC conferences in recent years have included more sessions on student welfare, including for those in the LGBTQ2S community who are often marginalized.

These efforts might appear to be only a drop in the bucket but I believe strongly that we must try. At GV Calgary, as I am sure is the case at most language programs, we observed care (or what is referred to as "pastoral care" in IALC) manifested by how people relate to each other in day-to-day interactions. Working in a language school or program is more than just a job for many. It is a helping profession where people can make a positive difference in the lives of others, even when they have experienced something horrendous. I am deeply sorry for what happened to the above-mentioned student in Calgary in 2014. I trust that I do not sound glib when I say that I sincerely hope that she was able to move on.

It seems cliched to say, but to take care of others, we need to care for ourselves. I have found that ratcheting up exercise helped me physically and mentally, allowing me to keep stress partially at bay. It was quite meditative to do laps of an indoor pool a couple of times a week. Of course, swimming is not for everyone but I encourage everyone to be physically active. I joke to my family that we all must be our own personal trainers.

I also believe that managers should not expect staff members to be workaholics or martyrs. I gently prodded staff and admonished myself, when we felt compelled to work through the day without a break or to eat lunch at our desks. I encouraged taking a minimum of a 10-minute-long walk outside or around the school. Professional organizations, such as Languages Canada and IALC, rightfully insist that their members articulate wellness policies (and of course safety protocols) in policy manuals for staff and orientation information for students, agents and host families. Like many managers, I have concluded that effective and efficient people, who take care of themselves and have reserves of mental and physical energy, are better able to care for others and to bounce back in times of adversity.

TIPS

If you are a teacher or an administrative staff member:

- Look for signs of stress among students and offer support with a light touch
- Weigh up the seriousness of student problems and be attuned to privacy issues
- Consider consulting with experienced staff
- Use whatever influence you have judiciously
- Take care of your own mental and physical wellbeing

If you are a manager:

- All the above, plus
- Ensure that you have questions about mental and health conditions on registration forms
- Clarify policies on wellness and safety with staff, homestay families and agents
- Communicate wellness and safety policies with students before they begin their studies
- Train staff to be vigilant and maintain a duty of care culture
- Communicate with other social service agencies, including the police, when warranted
- Maintain your values and search for common ground when considering and acting upon support and intervention strategies
- Encourage staff to take care of their own physical and mental wellness with explicit policies

2020

The rhythm of Global Village beat on. In January 2016, we marked twenty years of school operations in Calgary. We celebrated and ate cake in the school lounge with students and staff. I wondered about our next big anniversary, the twenty-fifth that would be in January 2021. I began to think about how and when to step back from day-to-day operations. But that was still far in the future. There were still good years to come and the usual ups and downs to challenge us all.

In May 2018, along with the persistent problem of the lone elevator being out of commission repeatedly, we had three incidents on consecutive Wednesdays when fire alarms were triggered. Twice they were false alarms. Nevertheless, each time the alarms were activated we had to evacuate the school. On one occasion, someone outside dropped a cigarette butt down a grate where papers ignited. A whole battalion of City of Calgary firefighters turned up with sirens blaring and in full battle uniforms. They searched the building until they found the source.

If that wasn't enough, the building managers scheduled the roof replacement for the month of July. They told us that they would use the "summer vacation period" to do the work. I pointed out that summer was our busiest time of year and most important to our business but it made no difference. They seemed entirely blind to our summer operations, which accommodated almost 300 students, five days a week as well as IELTS candidates on Saturdays. It was an ongoing dance to ensure that disruption to our classes and testing days was minimised.

Change was in the air again. In August 2018 a highly reputable UK-based group, the Centre for English Studies (CES) purchased GV Toronto, which was renamed CES Toronto. Going into 2018, I was a shareholder and member of the board of directors for both GV

Calgary and Victoria schools. I negotiated the sale of Cathie's and my shares in GV Calgary with GV Vancouver. Thus, by 2020, I remained a shareholder and director with GV Victoria but not in Calgary. I remained as Calgary's senior executive and continued to sit on the board of GV Marketing which was a separate entity from the schools.

The reputation of GV schools remained excellent, with quarterly school approval ratings consistently at 95 percent or higher in each location. We were deep into a period of global upheaval, fuelled by Trump, climate change and rising nationalism around the globe. The Trump Administration's hostile policies towards people from Mexico and the Middle East made America less appealing for international students. Due to disruptions in global economies, language programs everywhere became even more focussed on market share, profit margins and survival. Competition from the larger chain schools was becoming more aggressive as their venture capitalist owners sought to attract a greater market share of students.

Rumblings across the language industry, the changes within the GV group and the daily irritations that came with managing a language business all paled in comparison to what lay ahead. The word "unprecedented" has been over-used but it is still one of the best descriptors of what began impacting the entire world in March 2020.

The Canadian winter proceeded on its familiar trajectory early in 2020. By the time the Languages Canada Conference was held in Vancouver in the third week of February, people were anxious. We wondered aloud about the implications of the mysterious, deadly and highly infectious virus that had been first discovered in Wuhan, China. Some at the conference talked about dusting off the policies they had employed in the wake of SARS[22] back in 2003 or about H1N1[23] in more recent years.

---

22   Severe acute respiratory syndrome (SARS)
23   H1N1 also known as "swine flu"

Cathie and I had planned on taking a hiatus from our life in Calgary by travelling for two months starting in March 2020. However, we pulled the plug on the trip a few days before March 12. COVID-19 infections were increasing around the world. We held our breath about what would happen next in Canada. Far from edging away from the day-to-day business of GV Calgary, it became clear that I was going to have to work through the looming crisis.

We did not have long to wait. We ran our usual classes at GV Calgary on Friday, March 13 with no inkling that this would be the last day ever of onsite face-to-face language classes in the building. On Sunday, March 15, our Director of Programs Terry informed me that a student had been exposed to COVID-19.

Tania, Terry, and I had a long Sunday afternoon phone call. What to do next? The student did not know if she had COVID-19 herself. Her brother had done the responsible thing by informing the school of the risk. Comparatively little was known at that stage about the virus, except that it was highly virulent and transmissible. We couldn't place students or staff at risk, so we had to institute change, fast.

Terry had been working with teachers with the Zoom[24] online format. "Zoom", along with "unprecedented", "pandemic", "pivot" and "physical or social distancing", was going to be one of the most recognizable terms of 2020. Fortunately, Global Village schools in Canada had been aligning our curricula to a particularly good online language learning and teaching platform for several years. We took the hard decision that GV Calgary would discontinue face-to-face lessons and begin virtual lessons in real time on March 16. By March 17, GV Vancouver and GV Victoria had similarly pivoted. Across the globe, language schools unveiled a whole gamut of online offerings in the first weeks and months of the pandemic lockdowns. Within Global Village, the stellar efforts of instructors

---

24 Zoom Meetings (commonly shortened to Zoom) is a proprietary video teleconferencing software program developed by Zoom Video Communications Inc.

and academic directors meant that "GV Live" lessons were able to begin quickly.

With the rupture caused by the rapid onset of the pandemic in March 2020, everyone in any business had to adapt quickly. The language industry was greatly impacted as international travel and face-to-face class attendance was shut down. The key challenges of enrollment and revenues that concerned us prior to 2020, were thrown into starker contrast as we assessed the new and intimidating reality. Lots of unknowns clouded our thinking: closed borders, limited international flights, physical distancing, masking and fear. Estimates ranged from days to weeks to months concerning how long we would be locked down.

Along with the volatile unpredictability of the situation, a whole chorus of voices called out from many corners of Global Village. Over 25 years, along with many players, I had been through the set-up and start-up of Global Village Calgary, the relocation of the school, the renegotiation of leases, blizzards, even a flood and countless, seemingly intractable problems. The pandemic overshadowed all these.

The truth hit hard; the most challenging period of my working life was here and now with Global Village Calgary. I was no longer thinking of possible retirement but of months or even of years of sorting out this new puzzle. We had no idea what lay ahead. In the first weeks of the pandemic, I tried to take a reasoned approach to all that was happening with the business. I reminded myself that trying to maintain a positive attitude was going to be key over the long haul. No one had a business manual for this situation.

I cannot say enough in appreciation of how GV Calgary teachers, administrative staff as well as GV Marketing staff banded together. The same goes for GV Victoria, where administrative staff and teachers worked as a team in what was to be a prolonged period of adversity. GV administrative and marketing staff, as well as teachers, struggled mightily and successfully to support our agents and students and to keep classes going virtually. Through regular Zoom meetings, GV teachers in Calgary and Victoria met in parallel with our administrative teams in each location.

It wasn't long before other strong voices made their concerns known. The board members of the GV schools in Hawaii, Vancouver, Calgary and Victoria were understandably very worried about the future of the businesses. It was hard for all connected to GV to come to terms with fact that, what had been thriving businesses on Friday, March 13, were now businesses under threat. By the end of April, any thoughts that the lockdown would soon be lifted, had evaporated. Emergency board meetings took place for the school entities on a regular basis.

At GV Victoria, our landlord's representative was working cooperatively with the school on rent abatement because the building owner wished us to stay on as a tenant when our lease came up for renewal in September 2021. In contrast, at GV Calgary, the lease loomed as a major potential liability. While we had congratulated ourselves in 2017 on having negotiated a particularly good deal all the way to the end of December 2024, the lease was now a huge burden, with no formal rent abatement in sight. The federal wage subsidy program was certainly helping us make payroll. However, revenue coming into the school had been reduced to almost nothing in a shockingly short period.

Our schools in Calgary and Victoria managed to retain about 50 students in virtual, real-time classes throughout the spring of 2020 in comparison with our usual enrollment of over 200 students in each location. Although this number of students was good given the circumstances, this clearly wasn't going to be enough to sustain us.

I took regular bike rides along the Bow River Pathway as therapeutic exercise. It was hard to square the beautiful spring weather with the COVID-19 reality. I sincerely believed, and told the teachers and administrative staff, that I was confident that GV Calgary would survive. We had enough cash to last out the year if we scaled back operations, received rent concessions, and continued with wage subsidies. But I was headed for a comeuppance on my bullishness.

In the middle of May, two of our four Global Village schools announced that they were closing. GV Hawaii would later backtrack on that announcement when their owners found buyers for their business. GV Vancouver declared its intention to close on June 30. The decision of GV Vancouver to wind up its business had a knock-on effect on GV Calgary. Although the reality of the pandemic trumped everything, another salient fact was that GV Vancouver owned 60 percent of GV Calgary. Contrary to my expectations, it chose to totally close the books on the Vancouver business. It was complicated, but I should have seen this coming.

I tried to find some light in what felt like a black forest. I had several polite conversations with senior players at two of the larger chain schools about whether they each had any interest in purchasing GV Calgary. They were reluctant to take on the liability to do with the lease or that of staff salaries. The whole language industry was in a tailspin. Our chain competitors had their own financial battles as well as obvious directives from the venture equity companies that controlled them.

Following the news of the imminent closure of the Vancouver school, the three GV Vancouver board members who were also board members at GV Calgary resigned. Our school lawyer pointed out that this meant that it was up to the two remaining members of the board, as well as me as the senior executive officer, to decide what to do about GV Calgary. This was no time to be in denial.

I kept thinking about what the loss of employment would mean for more than thirty full-time employees at GV Calgary. Over those critical weeks, I would wake up before 3 a.m. and toss and turn about what could be done. I struggled mightily with the idea of closing the school.

We had to find the best way forward. Our accountant and facilities manager, Damon, produced numbers that showed we could ride out a prolonged spell with negligible revenue, if we received rent abatement and the wage subsidies continued. But the forecast was bleak if, as appeared entirely possible, the pandemic was to go through multiple waves continuing well into 2021 or even, perish the thought, beyond. One option for GV Calgary was to declare insolvency to protect the company against the huge concern about the liability which was potentially well over two million dollars on the lease that ran all the way up to the end of 2024.

It was time to be highly pragmatic. I accepted that the GV Calgary business was going to have to close and made the recommendation to the two board members, who agreed. I arrived at that conclusion through a process that was analogous to Kubler-Ross's[25] five stages of grief, which we had to come to grips with over a very intense period of just a few weeks.

In the week before the summer solstice on June 21, I let administrative staff and teachers know that GV Calgary would close its doors in the first week of August when the CELTA class ended. Our ESL virtual classes would end on July 31. GV Calgary students were offered continuing classes with GV Victoria teachers on the GV Live platform, and 20 students took up the offer.

Spring 2020 had reached its conclusion. It had begun with lockdowns around the world and global confusion. Initially, in our corner of the world, the messaging was unclear, both from the Canadian Federal Government about wearing masks and from the Alberta Provincial Government about the number of people allowed in a workspace. The resilience and character of the team at GV Calgary shone through, however. Our administrative staff and teachers were towers of strength to the community of students, test candidates and partners we served.

---

25 Elisabeth Kübler-Ross, *On Death and Dying* (1969)

Nevertheless, week by week since the onset of the pandemic, GV Calgary was forced to lay off more people. Then, at the end of July our school's last class for international students would be done. But there is more to closing a school than the last class. Not only are there the all too human considerations but there are stacks of furniture, libraries, computers and copiers to remove. There are legal and accounting concerns. There are memories to reconcile.

2020 continued its surreal trajectory as we entered summer. There was far less pedestrian and bike traffic on the Bow River Pathway. Downtown Calgary felt like a ghost town. Homeless people ambled around or sat disconsolately in the park across from the school. On my last days in the school, I reflected on how I used to look out my office window at this time of year and see GV Calgary's community with growing numbers of students at break times sitting in the park, taking advantage of the June warmth. I could picture students sitting with their classmates and new friends, sharing lunchtime. I remembered how I would go across to the park in the heat of summer to check on the teen students and staff. I also thought about the hilarity and exuberance on display at other times of the year when our Latin American students greeted their first experience of snow by frolicking in the park and throwing snowballs at each other.

The park features ten tall statues, all about 20 feet (6.5 m) high. Known as the *Brotherhood of Mankind*[26] and an impressive Calgary landmark, these were part of the British Pavilion at Expo 67. A Calgary industrialist had them brought to Calgary from Montréal to add to Calgary's public art collection. Sometimes students, especially on their graduation day from GV Calgary, liked to have their photos taken in front of the statues with the school's building as a backdrop.

It felt poignant to be in the school with these memories and just one or two other staff members, walking by our classrooms with

---

26   Mario Armengol, *Brotherhood of Mankind*. Part of the British Pavilion at Expo 67 in Montréal.

the row of chairs and desks sitting vacant. How empty and strange it was not to be running classes at GV Calgary. We also tried to get our heads around the fact that the Calgary Stampede, a tradition epitomizing summers in Calgary, had been cancelled for the first time since it started in 1912. COVID-19 forced the cancellations of the Calgary Folk Music Festival, the summer street festivals and other large gatherings.

The plan was to negotiate with the City of Calgary on giving up the lease and vacating the space by the end of August. Not only were we trying to navigate in unchartered waters about the lease, but Tania and I resolved to do all we could for staff in terms of termination packages. On both issues, I was very pleased to gain the full backing of the two board members with whom I had always worked very well. Now that positive working relationship really came into its own as we discussed the legal and other advice that I had received on dealing with the issues before us.

Over the years I learned to take lessons from the past and not fear but plan as well as possible for the future. Perspective is everything, I had learned the hard way. The ramifications of closing for all the school's employees and their families were life altering, however. Out of 36 full-time people, 20 of us had been on staff for more than 10 years. Out of the remaining 16 people, most had given as many as seven to nine years of service to the school. Moreover, there were also many part-time staff who came in to help on IELTS test days or were engaged in Cambridge CELTA teacher training.

In the last week of June, Tania and I met in person with some of the teachers and administrative staff. The meetings were a testament to the character of the sensitive and thoughtful staff team with whom we were associated at Global Village Calgary. Many asked how we were doing and acknowledged the difficulties that we had been facing in making extremely difficult decisions. We discovered that some staff were taking the time of the pandemic to reflect on where they were at with their lives and to make positive changes in terms of future career and lifestyle choices. Others were clearly struggling. It was heart-breaking to see. We had built a community and there was consolation in the fact that many staff members were friends and would stay in touch with each other.

For some, the school provided the strongest social connections in their lives. They would miss having GV Calgary to anchor them. Many commented on the excellence of GV Calgary students over the years and the values that we all held dear. Our most recent students registered at GV Calgary with identification numbers that started with 35,000. This meant that for more than 24 years, we had averaged more than 1,000 different students each year. The total number of students we had encountered was 50 percent higher than the capacity of the Calgary Flames indoor ice hockey arena or many professional football stadiums.

I continued to work through a settlement on the lease of the school's building with our landlord, the City of Calgary. The backing of the board members of GV Calgary was instrumental here as well. I was aided further by some good advice from our real-estate broker and a friend who had both worked with the City of Calgary years before and had been a board member on the Calgary Chamber of Commerce. For a reasonable settlement figure, the City of Calgary agreed to GV Calgary surrendering the lease and absolved the business of further lease obligations. That was a major milestone.

After my last day of meetings, I packed up a couple of boxes of my things in my office and paused in front of the school building. A brief thunderstorm, with large raindrops threatening to become hail, delivered a weather metaphor for a strange feeling of tumult rapidly giving way to peace. I felt the air clear.

Meanwhile, at Global Village Victoria we were staying alive. As in Calgary, there were herculean efforts made by staff in Victoria to ensure that the concerns and needs of students and agent partners were met. By October, I was the only remaining board member representing the interests of the shareholders. GV Marketing was also wrapped up.

Vancouver Island had held COVID-19 cases well in check. Thus, at GV Victoria, we had been able to re-start offering some face-to-face classes in July in a revamped format. The classes were held concurrently via web cams in the classroom enabling students both virtually and in class to mix. In offering this format, I recognized that we were expecting a lot of our teachers. IELTS and CELPIP[27] tests could also recommence at GV Victoria, with a greatly reduced capacity due to the need to maintain physical distancing.

As the board member, I worked with Paula who oversaw operations in Victoria. We were determined that Global Village would still have one school in Canada. "Survive then flourish" became our mantra. We headed up a management team, which included Jacqueline, our Director of Studies, and Kelly as Accounts Supervisor. Tania was brought in as well as Director of Testing Services to lend her experience with the management of the IELTS testing undertaken by GV Victoria. Redge in Calgary was hired to help coordinate the plethora of IELTS testing details. Carla, who had been Head Registrar at GV Calgary, was also an especially important addition to our Victoria administration team. With her experience and deft personal touch at managing agent partner and student relationships, she was going to help produce registrations which would be vital to GV Victoria's future. GV Victoria would continue.

Even though I was very much immersed in what was happening in GV Calgary and GV Victoria throughout the pandemic, I stayed in touch with colleagues in Languages Canada and in the International Association of Language Centres (IALC). People across the whole language industry, like the world at large, felt like they were living in a collective nightmare. The shutdown of international travel, along with all the other disruptions brought on

---

27   Canadian English Language Proficiency Index Program (CELPIP)

by the pandemic, not to mention all the uncertainty as to when this might all be over, meant that international educators were forced to cope as best they could. The public face of resilience shown by most people with whom I was communicating in the language business was impressive, given the seriousness and uncertainty around the global meltdown. Privately, colleagues I spoke with confirmed that every language program was hurting. The term "perfect storm" has also become a cliché. However, like most clichés there was a loud ring of clanging truth when it is applied to the language industry. An entire industry that depended on international travel was decimated in 2020.

In mid-October, Cathie and I travelled to Calgary from our new home in British Columbia's Okanagan. It had snowed and I made my way through the melting slush and semi-deserted streets of the downtown. A once-thriving city was hunkering down as winter was closing in again. "For lease" signs had appeared on many commercial properties. Calgary had already been badly impacted by the falling oil and gas prices prior to the pandemic. Now COVID-19 had delivered further hammer blows to the local economy and people's lives. Calgarians braced themselves against the cold outside and donned masks as they entered buildings. The city reflected an overall atmosphere of resignation that the pandemic was nowhere near over.

I met again with Tania and Damon to go over more details with the wind-up of the GV Calgary business, which would soon be officially dissolved. Leaving the downtown core, we drove past the North-West Travellers' Building[28] glinting in the sun. It was mid afternoon on a cold, clear autumn day. The Global Village and IELTS banners flapped in the breeze near street level. The painted lettering spelling out Global Village English Centres and our website address, high on the west and north sides of the exterior of the empty building, were still highly visible.

---

28   Alberta Register of Historic Places

TIPS

If you are a teacher or an administrative staff member:

- Be honest with students, colleagues and yourself in the face of uncertainties
- Don't wallow in negativity and try to be positive when reaching out to colleagues
- Take care of your own wellness
- Remember that core values can sustain you through a crisis

If you are a manager:

- All the above, plus
- Don't make bold statements that might need to be walked back
- Take the time to reflect and weigh up other options as well as the ones advised by experts
- Be pragmatic in the interests of the business and all those whom it serves when forced to decide its future
- Consult regularly with co-decision-makers, like board members
- Be clear in your communication
- Own your decision-making in crisis situations

Lessons Learned from Students

Those of us working at Global Village Calgary truly bought into the concept that our school was an international community learning together. Over the years, we observed that our students shared intense and often profoundly positive experiences that we hoped they would carry forward in their lives and careers. Personal connections forged in Calgary rippled out across the globe.

"Global Village[29]" was a term coined by Canadian Marshall McLuhan in the 1960s, along with his famous mantra, "the medium is the message"[30]. He claimed that individualism would be replaced by people identifying more with their "tribes", which would not be limited by international borders. McLuhan presciently foreshadowed the influence of the Internet and predicted that, increasingly, what is happening in one part of the world would immediately be communicated to others.

Saying that I have gained invaluable insights from international students in both informal and formal interactions does not do justice to their profound influence on my career. I have also found it useful in my work to bear in mind that everyone has a story and that many are going through personal upheavals because of events in their home countries and/or their shifting attitudes to their own place in the world.

I believe that international study is a force for expanding people's views of the world. For instance, female Saudi students who experience freedoms overseas may further question their limited rights when they return home. Of course, as an Aussie friend

---

29 Marshall McLuhan,*The Gutenberg Galaxy: The Making of Typographic Man* (1962)
30 Marshall McLuhan, *Understanding Media* (1964)

points out, countries that we may brand as oppressive say that we're trying to oppress them with our western culture and ideals.

In the last week of 2020, Canadian media again reported on the case of the Saudi woman, Loujain al-Hathloul, a graduate of the University of British Columbia in Vancouver, where she had also studied in an English language program. Upon her return to Saudi Arabia, she received a six-year prison sentence for speaking out in favour of basic women's rights, such as the right of women to drive. This right has actually been enacted in the Kingdom of Saudi Arabia since she was incarcerated.

On February 11, 2021 Canada's *Globe and Mail* daily newspaper reported her transition to home detention saying that Ms. al-Hathloul remained on probation and was barred from leaving Saudi Arabia for five years. Despite the tragic costs to Loujain al-Hathloul and her family, she is a very brave activist for change in her country. We might ask what role does international study in places like Canada play for a student such as Ms. al-Hathloul? We can reasonably surmise that learning English and completing a degree in a western country must have offered insights to this extraordinary, strong, young woman.

At GV Calgary, students often reported to me how much they appreciated their time in Canada. I was especially grateful when they dropped by my office for a chat during their last days. In speaking with many students and agents over the years, we were reminded time and again that whether students leave home with clear or unclear goals, they find that their studies lead them on surprising and life-affirming adventures.

Charbel Moreno, who worked as the Marketing Manager with Languages Canada from 2014 to 2017, was kind enough to share his story about his journey. Growing up in Mexico, he said there was a lot of awareness of the United States but not of Canada. However, he liked listening to Canadian popular music and decided that he would study in Canada, because he thought it would be affordable and offer him the opportunity to attain the English proficiency of a native speaker. Arriving in Halifax shortly after 9/11, his expectations were confirmed within a short time that living and studying in this Canadian city would be comfortable for him and fit his budget. He also bonded with his host couple, who like him were in their twenties and with whom he is good friends to this day.

Charbel reports that one day several months after moving to Halifax he had an epiphany, while riding a bus home from classes. The use of English around him had sounded like a muddle until that point. But now he understood what people sitting near him were saying about a movie. A further surprise awaited him when he returned to visit Mexico and found that he was "super homesick" for Canada. He had found his tribe and a life in Canada, especially when he met and married his wife, who was also from Mexico and had been a student in Vancouver. These days, Charbel works as a Recruitment Supervisor at the University of Toronto, where he says his work resonates with values that he describes as Canadian: harmony, peace and respect.

Charbel's story provides an insight into many of the best aspects of the language business. I found it important to remind myself about these insights and to learn about their backgrounds, as well as their orientations to study travel, by having regular conversations with students in the school. Even though marketing people like to speak about "products" in language programs, we are in fact providing "services" which have a very human dimension.

Whenever I greeted students, they usually responded instantly and warmly. I would ask them where they were from, what they did in their home countries and how long they would be at Global Village and in Canada. When prompted, students always shared something interesting about their backgrounds. A mature Brazilian student might tell me that she is a lawyer (sometimes pronounced like "liar" in Portuguese English!) and that she was using her four-week vacation to study in Calgary to improve her English.

I also learned important lessons from students, first as a teacher and then as a manager. I became aware that international students notice interpersonal aspects in schools, often in more ways than staff might expect. In a low context culture like Australia or Canada, where we explicate things more directly in a verbal manner, we also often show emotions on our faces and through physical gestures. Those of us working in language programs usually become attuned to students from other countries intuiting non-verbal signals with meaning.

In one of the early years of Global Village Calgary, a student wrote on a school survey, "Why do you look so serious, John? Please smile."

This was an instructive lesson for me from a student and served as a wake-up call. I resolved to try to show a more positive face around the school.

Interactions with students caused me ambivalence about Global Village schools' "English only" policy in the first years at GV Calgary when I wondered whether it was necessary. I kept these thoughts to myself, because "English only" was one of the ten commandments of GV. Of course, I could see the value of encouraging students to always use English in the school to help them make progress. Still, it was plain to see also that it went against the grain for students to deny a fundamental aspect of their culture, by being forced not to speak their native languages in social interactions around the school, especially when their English proficiency was minimal.

At GV Calgary, we focussed on positive reinforcement when students made efforts to use English in their break times. Students usually became allies of teachers and managers in the cause of maintaining the English language zone within the school, as it helped them with their proficiency.

I also learned in the first year of Global Village Calgary that my reluctant language policeman's role was fraught with misunderstanding. One day I said to a student that she would have to leave the school for the rest of the day, because she was consistently calling out to others across the student lounge in Korean. I was perplexed and embarrassed when she dropped to the floor in front of a few other students and clung to the hem of my pants and wailed, "Please don't make me go. Please don't make me go."

I quickly realized that she had registered the first part of what I had said, "You have to leave the school", but not the second part, "for the rest of the day". She thought I was expelling her from the school for good. When we cleared that up, she hurriedly jumped to her feet. I smoothed out the leg of my trousers and looked around nervously to see who had witnessed this thankfully brief incident.

When she graduated, we were able to laugh about it. But I was very wary after that about engaging with students publicly on contentious issues. I suspect that after we navigate through the worst of COVID-19, when schools get back to the business of more face-to-face classes, they will re-examine what is really important in their work and re-assess policies like "English only".

Even unhappy times with students can result in insights and teachable moments for both them and school staff. In the early years of GV Calgary, we had many incidents where we had to deal with students making poor decisions that bounced back on us. We learned that it was important not to over-react and to use humour when students tested us or their host families.

One day, after Lynn, our Assistant Director at the time, had challenged a group of Colombian students about constantly and loudly speaking Spanish in the school, one student put up a picture of his naked buttocks in the student lounge. Across "the bottom" of the picture of the mooning student was scrawled the message, "Here's to you, Lynn."

Hilariously, the student could be readily identified, because his distinctive watch could also be seen in the photo. At the monthly graduation, Lynn presented the mooning student with a certificate for "photographic excellence". All the Latin American students in the school got the joke.

The student smiled at Lynn and said, "You got me back pretty good."

One larger-than-life character at the time was Juan Duque, an 18-year-old from Colombia. In 1998 he led us on a merry dance. At times, he was akin to a one-man wrecking crew. One evening Lynn received a call from our Activities Coordinator, who said that Juan had been involved in a fight in a bar. Lynn went down there and dissuaded the bar owner from pressing charges.

Juan also made little effort to speak English in the school and teachers reported that he was disruptive in class. One day when Juan's mayhem had gone a little too far, I called him into my office. Juan slumped into a chair and looked at me like I was from a different planet. I assumed that he was acting out because he wanted to party with no holds barred in what he saw as the relatively unfettered environment of Calgary. He was also trying to come to terms with the political and social unrest in his country. We learned from his agent that his father was the mayor of a small city and that one of Juan's relatives had been kidnapped by FARC[31], the Colombian rebel group.

Despite an exuberant social life, Juan was making good strides with his English. He was clearly very bright as well as charismatic. He seemed emboldened by the fact that other students looked up to him. Slouching in my office, he began listing all the things that he thought were wrong with the school, as if he were an adversary making a list of demands.

I decided we needed to shift the paradigm. I invited Juan to switch seats with me, so that he was now looking at me from my side of the desk, while I acted like him and slumped back in the chair he had been in. Juan looked at me quizzically. He was clearly enjoying the attention yet wondering where this little role play would go.

---

31 Revolutionary Forces of Colombia (FARC)

I continued, "Now Juan, let's pretend that you are the manager of the language school instead of me. Now you must respond to me as if I am now the student, Juan Duque. You tell me how I should behave in the school and make the most of my time in Calgary."

After a light-hearted exchange, when he was just as bemused at my eccentricity in this conversation as I was with his antics in general, I pointed to my name on the door.

"OK Juan, can you answer a question for me? What is the name on the door?"

He shifted uncomfortably as he sensed a change of tone in the repartee. He responded slowly and sounded out my name as "Juan Taplin, Director of Programs."

"Right," I responded. "Juan Taplin. Not Juan Duque. Now, here is the deal. When you have your own school and it says Juan Duque on the door, then you can make the rules. And remember you will sometimes have to deal with difficult students. So you will need to be kind and patient."

He pursed his lips and nodded as if he was a goalie and I had just scored. We shook hands and I said, "Look, Juan, you are going to be a leader one day back in Colombia because you are already a leader here in the school. Please stay out of trouble and keep learning, AND stop giving the staff such a hard time, because we are all only trying to help you."

During the rest of his six months at the school, Juan did not exactly heed my words. He liked to stir things up. He was switched from homestay to homestay as he quickly exhausted the goodwill of each host family.

But there was a positive coda to our time with Juan. Seven years later in 2005, out of the blue, I received an email written in almost flawless English. It read:

Hello Mr. Taplin:

This is Juan Duque. I don't know if you remember me. In 1998, I studied at Global Village Calgary, or Rocky Mountain English Centre, as it was also called. I trust that you and Lynn are well.

I am now 25 years old and doing well in my city in Colombia. I have a good job in the field of International Economics, and my study time at your school helped me to use English well and to get a job. Now I have a good career and even a wife because I am married.

I also write to you because I want to apologize. When I was in Calgary, I had many troubling things in my life and I caused your school muchos problemas. I am sorry for that. You and Lynn treated me well in spite of all. I just want to say I remember you well and thank you for everything from the bottom of my heart.

Your student,

Juan Duque.

I was moved at the time, and it inspires me still. I think now, as I did when I received Juan Duque's email, that a lot of the work by a whole host of people associated with a language school goes unrecognized. How rare it was to receive an affirmation like this. The email was like a message from the universe to keep going. That did not just make my day; it made my month and even my year. It encouraged me to think beyond the daily grind about the real value of what we were doing.

I immediately forwarded the email to Lynn, who had moved on to a different career.

"Wow!" replied Lynn immediately. "Thanks for sharing, JT. Sometimes I miss international education so much."

In efforts to build community at GV Calgary, and because of lessons learned from students like Juan Duque, I felt that we needed to strive for more than just tolerance, which often comes across as begrudging acceptance. Tolerance is a reasonable fallback position, however, if there are worse options like hostility in play. I came to conclude that getting to know people in a real sense, even if interactions are fleeting or controversial, advances understanding and calms prejudicial stereotypes on all sides.

English novelist Ian McEwan said it exceedingly well in an essay for *The Guardian* newspaper just after September 11, 2001:

If the hijackers had been able to imagine themselves into the thoughts and feelings of the passengers, they would have been unable to proceed. Imagining what it is like to be someone other than yourself is at the core of our humanity. It is the essence of compassion, and it is the beginning of morality.

I believe that for most who have the opportunity, the international study experience is a hugely affirming force in their lives. Students go back out into their worlds, and often we hear nothing of them again. But we like to think we have helped in some way just to make them more informed about the world and its people, more acculturated or at least more tolerant, of course, better English speakers and hopefully global citizens in a more fully rounded sense.

Tips

If you are a teacher or administrative staff member:

- Remember that your words and demeanour are on display in work settings and have influence
- Be prepared to learn lessons from students who may challenge your assumptions
- Remind yourself that every student has a story and be present and listen
- Hold fast to the value of communicating authentically to build understanding
- Demonstrate empathy

If you are a manager:

- All the above, plus
- Be prepared to review policies that may not be as sacred as they seem
- Reflect and take the long view while attending to problems and issues
- Build a staff culture and school atmosphere that is professional and caring

Afterword

In May 2020, seven weeks into the coronavirus shutdown, I took a long walk around my wife's family's farm. A white Mother's Day had materialized out of another random Alberta spring snowstorm. It was on this snowy day that I decided to make better use of the early morning hours by writing about my Global Village days and other experiences as an educator.

I continued writing against the backdrop of the cycles of the pandemic and personal transitions. Cathie and I divided our time between Calgary and central British Columbia, where we continue to hunker down while the Omicron variant crests. We resolved not to waste time during the pandemic, despite the restrictions. We learned some lessons anew. Days pass as productive time when we are engaged and in the moment. People, life and nature do not stand still, and every stage of life is precious and transient.

Transitions in our lives and changing seasons reinforced these lessons. There is an old crabapple tree in our backyard in Calgary. I had a close-up view of it from our garage studio, where I would go to write most mornings as the COVID spring of 2020 unfolded. The small fruits from the tree are bitter, hard to process into something edible and definitely an acquired taste.

Throughout its annual cycle, I observed the crabapple tree's transition from winter dormancy to spring budding. It came out in full leaf and white blossoms in late May, dropping its flowers before the small green crabapples appeared. Through the summer the apples grew and thrived. Next, with the shortening days, fall hastened the next stage. The leaves dropped as the crabapples, ripe and red, lost their hardness with the frosts.

Just before spring 2019, I considered having the tree taken down. I was tired of the autumn ritual of cleaning up the splattered crabapples as they froze and softened. A few birds even got drunk on them as the weather cooled and the apples fermented. I had the local arborist in and was on the brink of having the tree lopped. But I pulled back at the last moment and I am glad I did. The arborist advocated to save the tree by saying, "You know there's lots of room in the sky for it to grow upwards."

He did a terrific job in trimming the tree. The crabapple tree is now 30 feet high and with the pruning and shaping, it has come back better than ever. It is quite therapeutic, as a meditative exercise, to clean up the soft crabapples over the last three or four months of each year, especially now that there are fewer of them.

Could the old crabapple tree be a metaphor for life and working in the language industry? After the pruning of many businesses and programs, the reinvention of the place of work in our lifestyles, and the enormous pain and dislocation caused by the pandemic, could the language industry come back better? Will it engage its participants more effectively? How can we survive and grow to flourish in the evolving landscape of international education and in our lives?

Naramata, British Columbia

January 2022

Acknowledgements

I thank the many people, too numerous to mention individually, who have influenced me throughout my career as an educator and lifelong learner. In particular, I note the efforts of teachers and other staff at Global Village and variously associated schools.

I also acknowledge the ongoing efforts of the many dedicated professionals who work in international education in all its formats across the world. A special shout goes out to the many agent partners as well as colleagues in Languages Canada and the International Association of Language Centres (IALC). Daily, you all make a positive difference in the lives of global citizens and act as a force for good in the world, even as the pandemic continues to shake the foundations of the language business. I encourage you to keep the faith!

I am especially grateful to Cathie Scott, Greg Stephenson, David Taplin, John George Taplin, John Wilson and Lynn Wyton, who reviewed early versions of chapters of this book and did not tell me to stop. Linda Auzins, Genevieve Bouchard, Cath D'Amico, Brent Doidge, Lisa Doolittle, Fred Greene, Terri Huck, Andrea Isfeld, Paula Jamieson, Maureen Ketcheson, Tania Knoch, Roger Leveque, Allison MacDonald, Charbel Moreno, Justin Quinn, Susan Scott, Bryan Smith, Robert Smith, Peter Taplin and David Wood all gave support to the project in various ways.

Sally Truss, my story editor and project manager, motivated me to reshape and focus, and guided the process of my dipping into the well of experience to come up with a streamlined version of my first manuscript. I also thank Ena Spalding, copy editor, and Jackie Bourgaize, designer.

My sincere gratitude to you all!

Finally, I acknowledge those who have passed, and left a profound legacy: my parents, Ann and Darcy Taplin, and my aunt, Beryl Taplin, who all instilled in me a thirst for education, respect for the Australian value that everyone deserves "a fair go", and an interest in the world at large. My thoughts and thanks also go to Cathie's parents, Evie and George Scott, and Cathie's aunt, Mary Trentham, who described themselves as "the last of the Prairie socialists". They accepted me unreservedly into their extended family and helped inspire my Canadian education and life.

Selected Bibliography

Armstrong, Jennifer Keishin. *Seinfeldia: How a Show About Nothing Changed Everything.* Simon and Shuster, 2016.

Babiak, Paul and Robert D. Hare. *Snakes in Suits*: Revised Edition. Harper Business, 2019.

Bridges, William and Susan Bridges. *Managing Transitions: Making the Most of Change.* Revised 25th Anniversary Edition, Cambridge: Da Capo Press, 2017.

Golding, William. *Lord of the Flies.* Faber and Faber, 1954.

Haggar, Mike. *Saudi human-rights activist released after 1,001 days in prison. The Globe and Mail.* February 11, 2021.

Heyman, Richard. *Why didn't you say that in the first place? How to be understood at work.* Jossey-Bass Publishers, 1994.

Hutchinson, Alex. *Endure: Mind, Body and the Curiously Elastic Limits of Human Performance.* William Morrow and Company, 2018.

Hune-Brown, Nicholas. *Students for Sale. The Walrus.* Volume 18, Number 6. September/October, 2021.

Ignatieff, Michael. *On Consolation: Finding Solace in Dark Times.* Random House, 2021.

Kahn, Elaine. *The Letters of Pierre Elliott Trudeau and Marshall McLuhan: Been Hoping We Might Meet Again.* Novalis, 2019.

Kim, W. Chan and Renée Mauborgne. *Blue Ocean Strategy: How to Create Uncontested Market Space and Make the Competition Irrelevant.* Harvard Business Review Press, 2004.

Kübler-Ross, Elisabeth. *On Death and Dying.* MacMillan, 1969.

Leszcz, Benjamin. *For Years, the office was not just the centre of work, but life itself. After COVID-19, let's change that.* The Globe and Mail. January 9, 2021.

Lodge, David. *Sense and Sensibility.* The Guardian. November 2, 2002.

McLuhan, Marshall. *The Gutenberg Galaxy: The Making of Typographic Man.* University of Toronto Press, 1962.

McLuhan, Marshall. *Understanding Media.* New American Library, 1964.

MacLennan, Hugh. *Two Solitudes.* Penguin, 1945.

Moreno, Charbel. Online interview with author about his experiences as an international student. October 26, 2021.

Patterson, Kerry, Joseph Grenny, Ron McMillan, and Al Switzler. *Crucial Conversations: Tools for Talking When Stakes Are High.* 2nd ed. McGraw Hill, 2012.

Pink Floyd, *The Wall*. Harvest and Columbia Records, 1979.

Scott, Cathie. "Partnership Theory of Canadian Health Systems: An Analysis of Theory and Practice". PhD dissertation, University of Calgary, 2001.

Scott-Taplin, Cathie. "The Development of Partnerships Among Community Agencies". Master's thesis, University of Calgary, 1993.

Seinfeld, Jerry. *Is this Anything?* Simon and Shuster, 2020.

Simpson, Ian. "Collaborative Curriculum Development". Master's thesis, University of Calgary, 1997.

Simpson, Ian, John Taplin, David Wood and Val Larsen. *Language as a Community Resource*. Alberta Culture and Multiculturalism, 1989.

Taplin, John G. "A Retrospective Cohort Study of Health Service Utilization and Costs of People Experiencing Homelessness Following Community Paramedic Care". Master's thesis, University of Calgary, 2021.

Taplin, John M. "Educational Policy and Alberta Immigrants". Master's thesis, University of Calgary, 1987.

Tsai, Bonnie. *Why We Swim*. Barnes and Noble, 2020.

Wood, David. "Universal Grammar in L2 Acquisition". Master's thesis, University of Calgary, 1989.

John M. Taplin

John Taplin is passionate about international and English language education. In this memoir of personal and business adventures, he shares his experiences as a teacher, teacher trainer, manager, and language school owner/director. John is known for his coordination of the international program at the University of Lethbridge before becoming founding director and later, President & CEO of Global Village Calgary.

Currently, John serves Global Village Victoria as Board Chair. John's professional interests include building resilience and capacity in language programs. He resides with Cathie, his wife, in Canada's Okanagan area.